Leveled Texts

For Fourth Grade

Consultants

Kristin Kemp, M.A.Ed.
Reading Level Consultant
Fenton, Missouri

Wendy Conklin, M.A.
Gifted Education Consultant
Round Rock, Texas

Dennis Benjamin
Special Education Consultant
Prince William County Public Schools, Virginia

Marcela von Vacano
English Language Learner Consultant
Arlington County Schools, Virginia

Publishing Credits

Corinne Burton, M.A.Ed., *President*; Conni Medina, M.A.Ed., *Managing Editor*; Emily Rossman Smith, M.A.Ed., *Content Director*; Angela Johnson, M.F.A., M.S.Ed., *Editor*; Robin Erickson, *Multimedia Designer*; Kevin Pham, *Production Artist*; Danielle Deovlet, *Assistant Editor*

Image Credits

pp.11, 13, 15 Greg Vaughn/VWPICS/Newscom; pp.18, 20, 22 20th Century Fox/MC Broom, Bruce/Album/Newscom; pp.24, 26, 28 LOC [LC-DIG-ggbain-38336]; pp.36, 38, 40 ChooseMyPlate.gov; pp.89, 91, 93 Ted Kinsman/Science Source; pp.102, 104, 106 LOC [4a27550]; pp.108, 110, 112 LOC [cph.3g07155]; pp.113, 115, 117 Wikimedia Commons; pp.114, 116, 118 Bibliothèque nationale de France; pp.125, 127, 129 NARA [542069]; pp.126, 128, 130 LOC [LC-U9-19271-33A]; All other images from iStock, Shutterstock, or the public domain.

Standards

Shell Education
A division of Teacher Created Materials
5301 Oceanus Drive
Huntington Beach, CA 92649-1030
http://www.tcmpub.com/shell-education
ISBN 978-1-4258-1631-5

Table of Contents

What Is Differentiation?

Over the past few years, classrooms have evolved into diverse pools of learners. Gifted students, English language learners, special-needs students, high achievers, underachievers, and average students all come together to learn from one teacher. The teacher is expected to meet their diverse needs in one classroom. It brings back memories of the one-room schoolhouse during early American history. Not too long ago, lessons were designed to be one size fits all. It was thought that students in the same grade learned in similar ways. Today, teachers know that viewpoint to be faulty. Students have different learning styles, come from different cultures, experience a variety of emotions, and have varied interests. For each subject, they also differ in academic readiness. At times, the challenges teachers face can be overwhelming, as they struggle to figure out how to create learning environments that address the differences they find in their students.

What is differentiation? Carol Ann Tomlinson (2014, 1) describes the challenge of differentiation as reaching out to "students who span the spectrum of learning readiness, personal interests, and culturally shaped ways of seeing and speaking about and experiencing the world." Differentiation can be carried out by any teacher who keeps the learners at the forefront of his or her instruction. The effective teacher asks, "What am I going to do to shape instruction to meet the needs of all my learners?" One method or methodology will not reach all students.

Differentiation encompasses what is taught, how it is taught, and the products students create to show what they have learned. When differentiating curriculum, teachers become the organizers of learning opportunities within the classroom environment. These categories are often referred to as content, process, and product.

- **Content:** Differentiating the content means to put more depth into the curriculum through organizing the curriculum concepts and structure of knowledge.
- **Process:** Differentiating the process requires the use of varied instructional techniques and materials to enhance the learning of students.
- **Product:** When products are differentiated, cognitive development and the students' abilities to express themselves improve.

Teachers should differentiate content, process, and products according to students' characteristics. These characteristics include students' readiness, learning styles, and interests.

- **Readiness:** If a learning experience aligns closely with students' previous skills and understanding of a topic, they will learn better.
- **Learning styles:** Teachers should create assignments that allow students to complete work according to their personal preferences and styles.
- **Interests:** If a topic sparks excitement in the learners, then students will become involved in learning and better remember what is taught.

How to Differentiate Using This Product

The leveled texts in this series help teachers differentiate language arts, mathematics, science, and social studies content for students. Each section has five passages, and each passage is written at three different reading levels. (See page 8 for more information.) While these texts are written on three reading levels, all levels remain strong in presenting subject-specific content and vocabulary. Teachers can focus on the same content standard or objective for the whole class, but individual students can access the content at their instructional levels rather than at their frustration levels.

Determining your students' instructional reading levels is the first step in the process. It is important to assess their reading abilities often so students are instructed on the correct levels. Below are suggested ways to use this resource, as well as other resources in your building, to determine students' reading levels.

- **Running records:** While your class is doing independent work, pull your below-grade-level students aside, one at a time. Individually, have them read aloud the lowest level of a text from this product (the circle level) as you record any errors they make on your own copy of the text. Assess their accuracy and fluency by marking the words they say incorrectly and listening for fluent reading. Use your judgment to determine whether students seem frustrated as they read. Following the reading, ask comprehension questions to assess their understanding of the material. If students read accurately and fluently and comprehend the material, move them up to the next level and repeat the process. As a general guideline, students reading below 90% accuracy are likely to feel frustrated as they read. There are also a variety of published reading assessment tools that can be used to assess students' reading levels using the oral running record format.
- **Refer to other resources:** You can also use other reading level placement tests, such as the Developmental Reading Assessment or the Qualitative Reading Inventory, to determine your students' reading levels. Then, use the chart on page 8 to determine which text level is the best fit for each student.

Teachers can also use the texts in this series to scaffold the content for their students. At the beginning of the year, students at the lowest reading levels may need focused teacher guidance. As the year progresses, teachers can begin giving students multiple levels of the same text to allow them to work independently to improve their comprehension. This means that each student would have a copy of the text at his or her independent reading level and a copy of the text one level above that. As students read the instructional-level texts, they can use the lower texts to better understand the difficult vocabulary. By scaffolding the content in this way, teachers can support students as they move up through the reading levels. This will encourage students to work with texts that are closer to the grade level at which they will be tested.

General Information About Student Populations

Below-Grade-Level Students

As with all student populations, students who are below grade level span a spectrum of abilities. Some of these students have individualized education plans, while others do not. Some below-grade-level students are English language learners (ELLs), while others are native English speakers. Selected students receive intervention and/or support services, while many other students do not qualify for such services. The shift toward inclusive classrooms has caused an increase in the number of below-grade-level students in the general education classrooms.

These students, regardless of abilities, are often evaluated on the same learning objectives as their on-grade-level peers, and their learning becomes the responsibility of classroom teachers. The following questions come to mind: How do classroom teachers provide this population with "access to texts that allows them to perform like good, proficient readers" (Fountas and Pinnell 2012, 2)? How do classroom teachers differentiate for this population without limiting access to content, grade-level vocabulary, and language? Pages 132–136 give tangible strategies to support this student population.

On-Grade-Level Students

Often, on-grade-level students get overlooked when planning curriculum. More emphasis is placed on students who struggle and, at times, on those students who excel. Teachers spend time teaching basic skills and even go below grade level to ensure that all students are up to speed. While this is a noble thing and is necessary at times, in the midst of it all, the on-grade-level students can get lost in the shuffle. Providing activities that are too challenging can frustrate these students, and on the other hand, assignments that are too easy can seem tedious. The key to reaching this population successfully is to find the right level of activities and questions while keeping a keen eye on their diverse learning styles. Strategies can include designing activities based on the theory of multiple intelligences. Current brain research points to the success of active learning strategies. These strategies provoke strong positive emotions and use movement during the learning process to help these students learn more effectively. On-grade-level students also benefit from direct teaching of higher-level thinking skills. Keep the activities open ended so that these students can surprise you with all they know. The strategies described on pages 137–138 were specifically chosen because they are very effective for meeting the needs of on-grade-level students.

General Information About Student Populations *(cont.)*

Above-Grade-Level Students

All students should be learning, growing, and expanding their knowledge in school. This includes above-grade-level students, too. But they will not grow and learn unless someone challenges them with appropriate curriculum. In her article "Differentiating the Language Arts for High Ability Learners," Joyce Van Tassel-Baska (2003, 2) stresses that "the level of curriculum for gifted learners must be adapted to their needs for advancement, depth, and complexity." Doing this can be overwhelming at times, even for experienced teachers. However, there are some strategies that teachers can use to challenge the gifted population. These strategies include open-ended questions, student-directed learning, and extension assignments. See pages 139–140 for more information about each of these strategies.

English Language Learners

Acquiring a second language is a lengthy process that integrates listening, speaking, reading, and writing. Students who are newcomers to the English language are not able to deeply process information until they have mastered a certain number of language structures and vocabulary words. Even after mastering these structures, English language learners need to be immersed in rich verbal and textual language daily in school. Students may learn social language in one or two years. However, academic language takes up to eight years for most students to learn. Teaching academic language requires good planning and effective implementation. Pacing, or the rate at which information is presented, is another important component in this process. English language learners need to hear the same words in context several times, and they need to practice structures to internalize the words. Reviewing and summarizing what was taught are absolutely necessary for English language learners' success in the future (August and Shanahan 2006). See pages 141–143 for more information about each of the strategies mentioned here.

How to Use This Product

Readability Chart

Title of the Text	Circle	Square	Triangle
Excerpt from *Anne of Green Gables*	2.9	4.5	6.2
Excerpt from *The Story of Dr. Dolittle*	2.7	4.3	6.0
History's Mysteries	2.9	4.7	6.3
Go-Kart Racing	2.9	4.5	6.5
Food Groups	2.9	4.5	6.4
Eco-Predictions	2.7	4.7	6.4
Journeys: Land, Air, Sea	2.7	4.3	6.0
Patterns Around Us	2.9	4.8	6.3
All About Sharks	2.9	4.8	6.5
The Bread Book	2.7	4.3	6.2
Producers and Consumers	2.9	4.7	6.3
The Nutrient Cycle	2.9	4.6	6.2
Circuits	2.8	4.5	6.1
Sound Waves and Communication	2.9	4.6	6.1
The Story of Fossil Fuels	2.8	4.7	6.4
Pocahontas	2.8	4.5	6.5
Life in the Colonies	2.9	4.5	6.2
Marie Antoinette	2.9	4.7	6.0
Lewis and Clark	2.9	4.8	6.6
Dr. Martin Luther King Jr.	2.9	4.7	6.5

Correlation to Standards

The Every Student Succeeds Act (ESSA) mandates that all states adopt challenging academic standards that help students meet the goal of college and career readiness. While many states already adopted academic standards prior to ESSA, the act continues to hold states accountable for detailed and comprehensive standards.

Shell Education is committed to producing educational materials that are research and standards based. In this effort, all products are correlated to the academic standards of the 50 states, the District of Columbia, and the Department of Defense Dependent Schools. Shell Education uses the Mid-continent Research for Education and Learning (McREL) Compendium to create standards correlations. Each year, McREL analyzes state standards and revises the compendium. By following this procedure, they are able to produce a general compilation of national standards. A correlation report customized for your state can be printed directly from the following website: **www.tcmpub.com/administrators/correlations/**.

How to Use This Product *(cont.)*

Components of the Product

Go-Kart Racing

The Leveled Texts

- There are 20 topics in this book. Each topic is leveled to three different reading levels. The images and fonts used for each level within a topic are the same.
- Behind each page number, you'll see a shape. These shapes indicate the reading levels of each piece so that you can make sure students are working with the correct texts. The reading levels fall into the ranges indicated below. See the chart on page 8 for the specific level of each text.

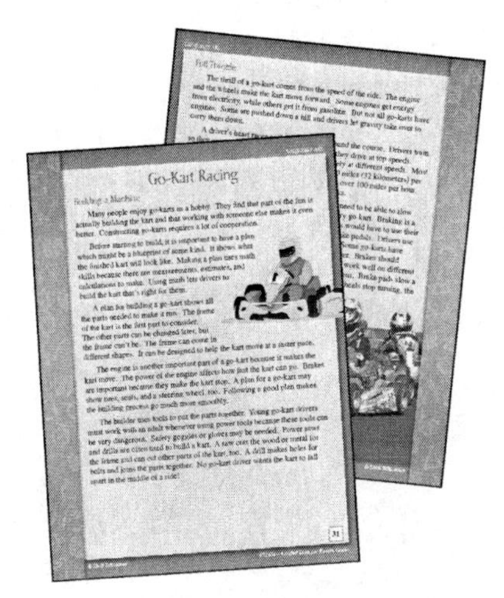

Go-Kart Racing

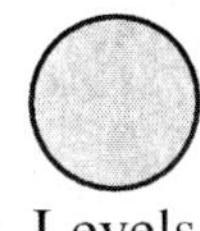		
Levels 2.7–2.9	Levels 4.3–4.8	Levels 6.0–6.6

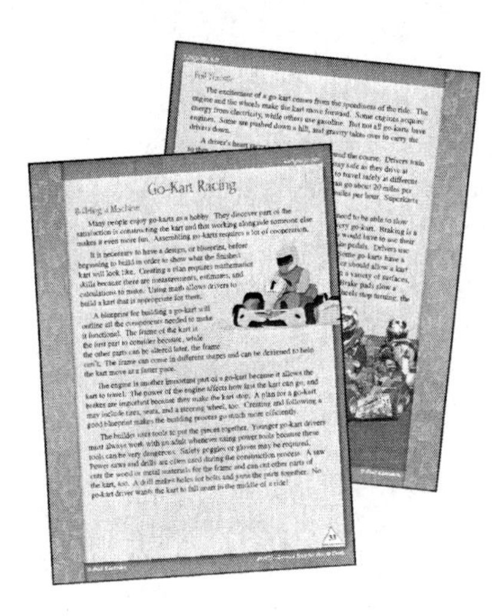

Go-Kart Racing

Comprehension Questions

- Each level of the texts includes a comprehension question. Like the texts, the comprehension questions were leveled by an expert. They are written to allow all students to be successful within a whole-class discussion. The questions are closely linked so that teachers can ask multiple questions on the topics and all students will be able to participate in the conversations about the texts. The below-grade-level students might focus on the facts, while the above-grade-level students can delve deeper into the meanings of the texts.

How to Use This Product *(cont.)*

Tips for Managing the Product

How to Prepare the Texts

- When you copy these texts, be sure you set your copier to copy photographs. Run a few test pages and adjust the contrast as necessary. If you want the students to be able to appreciate the images, you will need to carefully prepare the texts for them.
- You also have full-color versions of the texts provided in PDF form on the Digital Resource CD. (See page 144 for more information.) Depending on how many copies you need to make, printing full-color versions and/or copying from a full-color version might work best for you.
- Keep in mind that you should copy two-sided to two-sided if you pull the pages out of the book. The shapes behind the page numbers will help you keep the pages organized as you prepare them.

Distributing the Texts

- Some teachers wonder about how to hand out the texts within one classroom. They worry that students will feel insulted if they do not get the same papers as their neighbors. The first step in dealing with these texts is to set up your classroom as a place where all students learn at their individual instructional levels. Making this clear as a fact of life in your classroom is key. Otherwise, the students may constantly ask about why their work is different. You do not need to get into the technicalities of the reading levels. Just state it as a fact that every student will not be working on the same assignment every day. If you do this, then passing out the varied levels is not a problem. Just pass them to the correct students as you circle the room.
- If you would rather not have students openly aware of the differences in the texts, you can try these strategies for passing out the materials.
    - Make a pile in your hands from the circle to triangle level. Put your fingers between the levels. As you approach each student, you pull from the correct section to meet his/her reading level. If you do not hesitate too much in front of each desk, the students will probably not notice.
    - Begin the class period with an opening activity. Put the texts in different places around the room. As students work quietly, circulate and direct students to the correct locations for retrieving the texts you want them to use.
    - Organize the texts in small piles by seating arrangement so that when you arrive at a group of desks, you will have just the levels you need.

Excerpt from *Anne of Green Gables*

By Lucy Maud Montgomery

It was dark when supper was ready. Still there was no sign of Anne. Marilla washed and put away the dishes grimly. She wanted a candle to light her way down to the cellar. So she went up to the east gable for the one that usually stood on Anne's table. Lighting it, she turned around to see Anne herself lying on the bed. She was facedown among the pillows.

"Mercy on us," said the astonished Marilla. "Have you been asleep, Anne?"

"No," was the muffled reply.

"Are you sick then?" demanded Marilla anxiously. She went over to the bed.

Anne sank deeper into her pillows. It was as if she were trying to hide herself from view.

"No, but please, Marilla, go away. Don't look at me. I'm in the depths of despair. I don't care who gets ahead in class or writes the best essay. Or even who sings in the Sunday school choir. Little things like that are of no importance now. I don't suppose I'll ever be able to go anywhere again. My career is done. Please, Marilla, go away and don't look at me."

"Did anyone ever hear the like?" the puzzled Marilla wanted to know. "Anne Shirley, whatever is the matter with you? What have you done? Get up and tell me. There now, what is it?"

Anne had slid to the floor in weary obedience. "Look at my hair, Marilla," she whispered.

Accordingly, Marilla lifted her candle and looked suspiciously at Anne's hair. It was flowing in heavy masses down her back. It certainly had a very strange appearance.

"Anne Shirley, what have you done to your hair? Why, it's GREEN!"

Green it might be called—a strange, dull, bronzy green. It still had streaks here and there of the original red to heighten the ghastly effect. Never in all her life had Marilla seen anything so grotesque as Anne's hair at that moment.

"Yes, it's green," moaned Anne. "I thought nothing could be as bad as red hair. But now I know it's ten times worse to have green hair. Oh, Marilla, you little know how utterly wretched I am."

"I little know how you got into this fix. But I mean to find out," said Marilla. "I've been expecting something for some time. You haven't got into any scrape for over two months. I was sure another one was due. Now, then, what did you do to your hair?"

"I dyed it."

"Dyed it! Dyed your hair! Anne Shirley, didn't you know it was a wicked thing to do?"

"Yes, I knew it was a little wicked," admitted Anne. "But I thought it was worthwhile. Just a little wicked to get rid of red hair. Besides, I meant to be extra good in other ways. That would make up for it."

Think About It!

Why was Anne hiding in her room?

Excerpt from *Anne of Green Gables*

By Lucy Maud Montgomery

It was dark when supper was ready, and still there was no sign of Anne. Marilla washed and put away the dishes grimly. Then, wanting a candle to light her way down to the cellar, she went up to the east gable for the one that usually stood on Anne's table. Lighting it, she turned around to see Anne herself lying on the bed, face downward among the pillows.

"Mercy on us," said the astonished Marilla, "have you been asleep, Anne?"

"No," was the muffled reply.

"Are you sick then?" demanded Marilla anxiously, going over to the bed.

Anne sank deeper into her pillows as if trying to hide herself forever from mortal eyes.

"No, but please, Marilla, go away and don't look at me. I'm in the depths of despair, and I don't care who gets ahead in class or writes the best composition or sings in the Sunday school choir anymore. Little things like that are of no importance now because I don't suppose I'll ever be able to go anywhere again. My career is done. Please, Marilla, go away and don't look at me."

"Did anyone ever hear the like?" the mystified Marilla wanted to know. "Anne Shirley, whatever is the matter with you? What have you done? Get right up this minute and tell me. This minute, I say. There now, what is it?"

Anne had slid to the floor in despairing obedience. "Look at my hair, Marilla," she whispered.

Accordingly, Marilla lifted her candle and looked suspiciously at Anne's hair, flowing in heavy masses down her back. It certainly had a very strange appearance.

"Anne Shirley, what have you done to your hair? Why, it's GREEN!"

Green it might be called—a strange, dull, bronzy green, with streaks here and there of the original red to heighten the ghastly effect. Never in all her life had Marilla seen anything so grotesque as Anne's hair at that moment.

"Yes, it's green," moaned Anne. "I thought nothing could be as bad as red hair. But now I know it's ten times worse to have green hair. Oh, Marilla, you little know how utterly wretched I am."

"I little know how you got into this fix, but I mean to find out," said Marilla. "I've been expecting something for some time. You haven't got into any scrape for over two months, and I was sure another one was due. Now, then, what did you do to your hair?"

"I dyed it."

"Dyed it! Dyed your hair! Anne Shirley, didn't you know it was a wicked thing to do?"

"Yes, I knew it was a little wicked," admitted Anne. "But I thought it was worthwhile to be a little wicked to get rid of red hair. Besides, I meant to be extra good in other ways to make up for it."

Think About It!

Why did Anne dye her hair?

Excerpt from *Anne of Green Gables*

By Lucy Maud Montgomery

It was dark when supper was ready, and still there was no sign of Anne. Marilla washed and put away the dishes grimly. Then, desiring a candle to light her way down to the cellar, she went up to the east gable for the one that was generally located on Anne's table. Lighting it, she turned around to notice Anne herself lying on the bed, face downward among the pillows.

"Mercy on us," said the astonished Marilla, "have you been asleep, Anne?"

"No," was the muffled reaction.

"Are you sick then?" demanded Marilla anxiously, going over to the bed.

Anne descended deeper into her pillows as if trying to hide herself for eternity from mortal eyes.

"No, but please, Marilla, depart from here and don't look at me. I'm in the depths of despair, and I don't care who gets ahead in lessons or transcribes the finest composition or harmonizes in the Sunday school choir any more. Minuscule things like that are of no significance now because I don't suppose I'll ever be able to go anywhere again. My career is over, so please, Marilla, go away and don't gaze upon me."

"Did anyone ever hear the like?" the mystified Marilla wanted to know. "Anne Shirley, whatever is the matter with you? What have you done? Get right up this minute; there now, what is it?"

Anne had slithered to the floor in despairing obedience and whispered, "Look at my hair, Marilla."

Accordingly, Marilla lifted her candle and looked suspiciously at Anne's hair, flowing in heavy masses down her back. It certainly had a very peculiar appearance.

"Anne Shirley, what have you done to your hair . . . why, it's GREEN!"

Green it might be called—a strange, dull, bronzy green, with splashes here and there of the original red to heighten the ghastly effect. Never in all her life had Marilla seen anything so grotesque as Anne's hair at that moment.

"Yes, it's green," lamented Anne. "I thought nothing could be as terrible as being redheaded. But now I know green hair is ten times worse. Marilla, you little know how utterly wretched I am."

"I little know how you got into this catastrophe, but I mean to find out," said Marilla. "I've been expecting something for some time. You haven't got into any predicament for over two months, and I was certain another one was due. Now, then, what did you do to your hair?"

"I dyed it."

"Dyed it! Anne Shirley, didn't you know it was a wicked thing to do?"

"Yes, I knew it was a little wicked," admitted Anne, "but I thought it was worthwhile to be a little wicked to be liberated of red hair. I meant to be especially good in other ways to make up for it."

Think About It!

Describe Anne's personality.

Excerpt from *The Story of Dr. Dolittle*

By Hugh Lofting

A Message from Africa

That winter was a very cold one. One night in December, all the animals were sitting round the warm fire in the kitchen. The Doctor was reading aloud to them out of books he had written himself in animal language. The owl, Too-Too, suddenly said, "Sh! What's that noise outside?"

They all listened, then, they heard the sound of someone running. The door flew open. Chee-Chee, the monkey, ran in, badly out of breath.

"Doctor!" he cried, "I've just had a message from a cousin of mine in Africa. There is a terrible sickness among the monkeys out there. They are all catching it. They are dying in hundreds. They have heard of you. They beg you to come to Africa to stop the sickness."

"Who brought the message?" asked the Doctor. He took off his glasses and lay down his book.

"A swallow," said Chee-Chee. "She is outside on the rain barrel."

"Bring her in by the fire," said the Doctor. "She must be frozen with the cold. Her kind flew south six weeks ago!"

So the swallow was brought in. She was all huddled and shivering. Though she was a little afraid at first, she soon got warmed up. She sat on the edge of the mantel and began to talk.

When she had finished, the Doctor spoke. "I would gladly go to Africa. The trip would be especially nice in this bitter weather. But I'm afraid we don't have enough money to buy the tickets. Get me the money box, Chee-Chee."

So the monkey climbed up the dresser. He got it off the top shelf. There was nothing in it. Not one single penny!

"I felt sure there was two pence left," said the Doctor.

"There was," said the owl. "But you spent it. You bought a rattle for that badger's baby when he was teething."

"Did I?" said the Doctor. "Dear me, dear me! What a pain money is, to be sure! Well, never mind. I will go down to the seaside. Perhaps I shall be able to borrow a boat that will take us to Africa. I knew a seaman once who brought his baby to me with measles. Maybe he'll lend us his boat—after all, the baby got well."

So early the next morning, the Doctor went down to the seashore. When he came back, he told the animals it was all right. The sailor would lend them the boat.

The crocodile, monkey, and parrot were very glad and began to sing. They were going back to Africa, their real home!

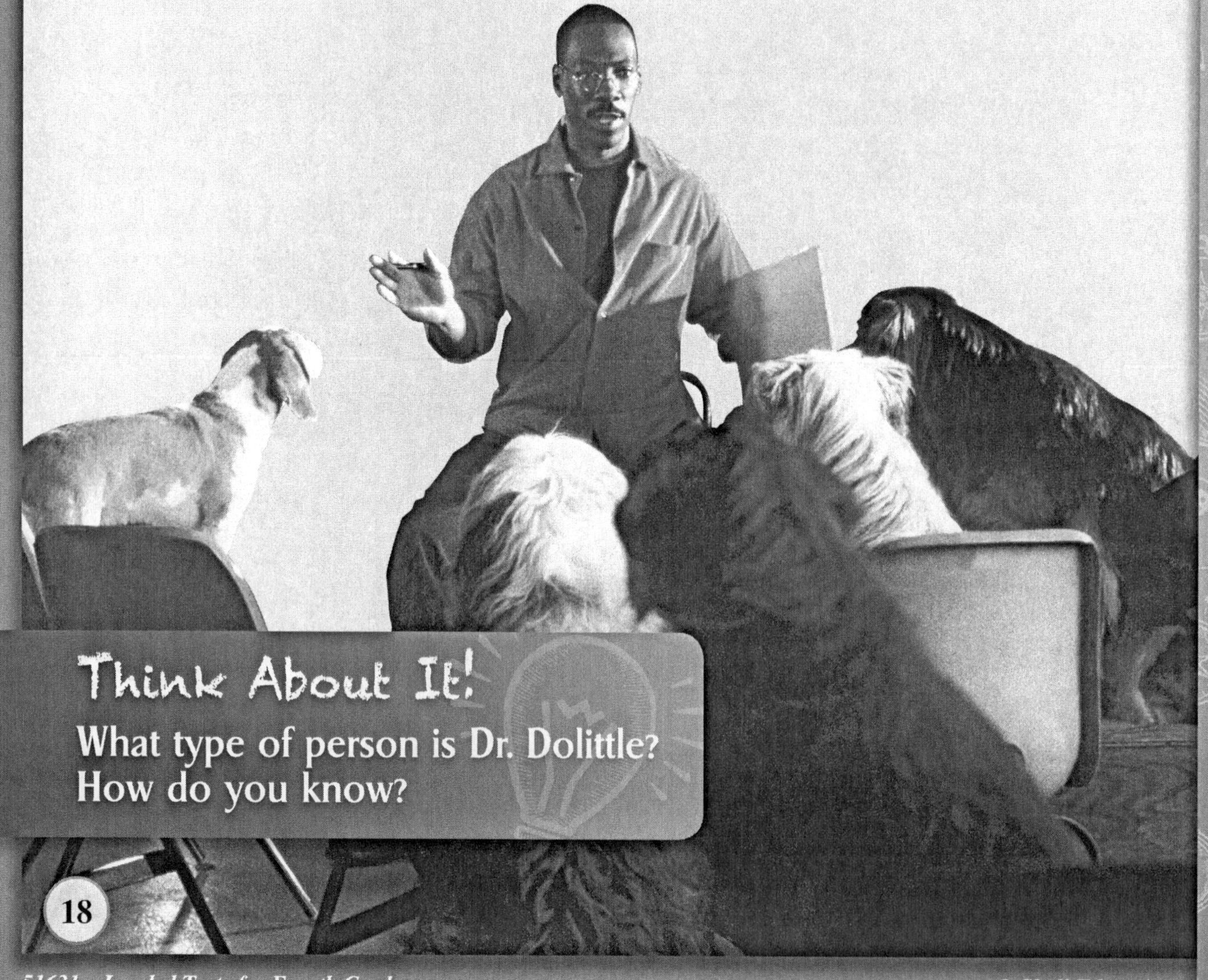

Think About It!

What type of person is Dr. Dolittle? How do you know?

Excerpt from *The Story of Dr. Dolittle*

By Hugh Lofting

A Message from Africa

That winter was a very cold one. One night in December all the animals were sitting round the warm fire in the kitchen, the Doctor was reading aloud to them out of books he had written himself in animal language. Suddenly the owl, Too-Too, said, "Sh! What's that noise outside?"

They all listened, and presently, they heard the sound of someone running. The door flew open, and the monkey, Chee-Chee, ran in, badly out of breath.

"Doctor!" he cried, "I've just had a message from a cousin of mine in Africa. There is a terrible sickness among the monkeys out there. They are all catching it—and they are dying in hundreds. They have heard of you, and beg you to come to Africa to stop the sickness."

"Who brought the message?" asked the Doctor, taking off his spectacles and laying down his book.

"A swallow," said Chee-Chee. "She is outside on the rain barrel."

"Bring her in by the fire," said the Doctor. "She must be frozen with the cold. The swallows flew south approximately six weeks ago!"

So the swallow was brought in; all huddled and shivering. Although she was a little afraid at first, she soon got warmed up, sat on the edge of the mantelpiece and began to talk.

When she had finished, the Doctor said, "I would gladly go to Africa—especially in this bitter weather. But I'm afraid we haven't money enough to buy the tickets. Get me the money box, Chee-Chee."

So the monkey climbed up and got it off the top shelf of the dresser. There was nothing in it—not one single penny!

"I felt sure there was two pence left," said the Doctor.

"There was," said the owl. "But you spent it on a rattle for that badger's baby when he was teething."

"Did I?" said the Doctor. "Dear me, dear me! What a nuisance money is, to be sure! Well, never mind. Perhaps if I go down to the seaside, I shall be able to borrow a boat that will take us to Africa. I knew a seaman once who brought his baby to me with measles. Maybe he'll lend us his boat—since the baby got well."

So early the next morning, the Doctor went down to the seashore. And when he came back, he told the animals it was all right—the sailor was going to lend them the boat.

At the news the crocodile, monkey, and parrot were very glad and began to sing because they were going back to Africa, their real home.

Think About It!

Why doesn't Dr. Dolittle have any money? What does this tell you about him?

Excerpt from *The Story of Dr. Dolittle*

By Hugh Lofting

A Message from Africa

That winter was a very blustery one. One evening in December, all of the animals were sitting round the cozy fire in the kitchen. The Doctor was reading aloud to them out of books he had written himself in animal language. Suddenly, the owl, Too-Too, said, "Sh! What's that noise outside?"

They all listened, and presently they heard the sound of someone running. Then the door flew open, and the monkey, Chee-Chee, sprinted in, terribly out of breath.

"Doctor!" he cried, "I've just received a message from a cousin of mine in Africa. There is a terrible epidemic among the monkeys out there. They are all catching it—and they are perishing in hundreds. They have heard of you, and beg you to travel to Africa to eradicate the sickness."

"Who delivered the message?" asked the Doctor, taking off his spectacles and laying down his book.

"A swallow," said Chee-Chee, "and she is outside on the rain barrel."

"Quickly, bring her by the fire," instructed the Doctor. "She must be quivering with the cold. The swallows flew south six weeks ago!"

So the swallow was brought in, all huddled and shivering; and although she was a little frightened at the beginning, she soon warmed up. Delicately perched on the edge of the mantelpiece she began to converse.

When she had finished, the Doctor said, "I would gladly sojourn to Africa—especially in this bitter weather. But I'm afraid we haven't money enough to purchase the tickets. Retrieve the money box, Chee-Chee."

So the monkey began climbing and got it off the uppermost shelf of the dresser. There was nothing in it—not one solitary penny!

"I felt positive there was two pence left," said the Doctor.

"There was," said the owl, "but you spent it on a rattle for that badger's baby when he was teething."

"Did I?" said the Doctor. "Dear me, dear me, what a nuisance money is, to be sure! Well, never mind, because perhaps if I travel down to the seaside, I shall be able to borrow a boat that will ferry us to Africa. I was acquainted with a seaman once who brought his baby to me with measles. Maybe he'll lend us his boat—since the baby got well."

So early the next morning, the Doctor went down to the seashore, and when he came back, he told the animals it was all right—the sailor was going to lend them the boat.

Then, in jubilee, the crocodile, monkey, and parrot began to sing because they were going back to Africa, their genuine home.

Think About It!

Do you think Dr. Dolittle will help the monkeys in Africa?

History's Mysteries

Masked Prisoner

A mystery man was in jail in France from around 1669 until he died in 1703. Most of the time, he was in the Bastille. No one ever saw the man's face. It was always covered with a black velvet mask. The prisoner's name was Eustache Dauger. That is most likely not his real name. Dauger could not talk about himself. If he did, he would have been killed. Only the head of the Bastille was allowed to see his face. No one knows who he was. No one knows why he was jailed. Many people believe he was the brother of King Louis XIV. He may have even been a twin brother. They think Louis XIV jailed him. With him jailed, no one could stop Louis from being king.

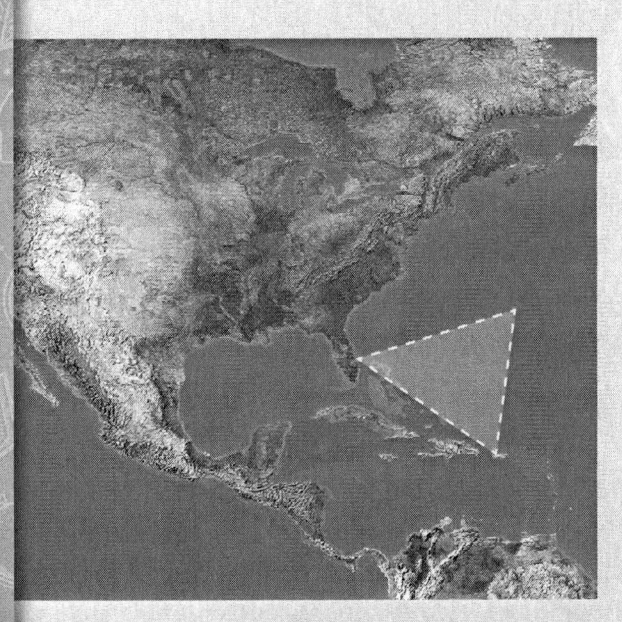

Vanishing Act

The Bermuda Triangle is a strange place. It is in the Atlantic Ocean. Dozens of boats, planes, and people have vanished there. Some people think it is not safe. They think there is a magnetic field that can make a compass stop working. Others blame bad weather. There are strong water currents.

In 1918, a U.S. Naval ship went missing. It left the island of Barbados. It went into the Triangle. The ship vanished without a trace. The crew of 306 people vanished too. Some people blame storms. If it were storm related the ship or the crew would have been found. Some blame war enemies. Because no remains have been found the mystery is still unsolved.

In 1945, five U.S. Navy bombers left Florida. They flew out on a training flight. The pilots got lost in the Triangle. The Navy could hear one pilot's radio. The leader said his compass was off. He said things looked strange. And he couldn't figure out where they were. A sixth plane was sent to find them. All of the planes vanished. The Navy called for help. They were to look for the missing planes. But no trace of them was ever found.

Anastasia

There was big trouble in Russia in the early 1900s. Russians wanted to get rid of their old rulers. Nicholas II was the ruler at the time. He was married. He had five children. Anastasia was his youngest daughter. On July 17, 1918, the secret police came. They killed Nicholas and his family. But did Anastasia survive? For years, many people thought so. Some women claimed to be the missing girl. They each stepped forward. They wanted the family fortune. But in 2009, science proved them all wrong. It is sure that the whole family died that day.

Bigfoot

Some people who live in the Pacific Northwest say they have seen a strange thing. It is a giant, apelike, wild man! They say he roams the forest. They claim he walks on two legs. He is more than seven feet tall. He has huge feet. Some people have photos of a giant, apelike man. But no one can tell if it is a real creature. Maybe it's just a person in an ape suit! Some scientists think Bigfoot may be real.

Bigfoot is also called *Sasquatch*. This comes from a Salish Indian word. It means "wild man." Native people lived in the Pacific Northwest. They told stories of wild men for hundreds of years. Then the stories were written down. J. W. Burns wrote them down in the 1920s. He was the first to call the creature *Sasquatch*.

Think About It!

Why are these historical events considered mysteries?

History's Mysteries

Masked Prisoner

From around 1669 until his death in 1703, a mystery man was held in jails in France. Most of the time, he was in the Bastille. No one ever saw the man's face. It was always covered with a black velvet mask. The prisoner's name was Eustache Dauger. That is probably not his real name. Dauger was told he could not talk about himself. If he did, he would have been killed. Only the head of the Bastille was allowed to see his face. No one knows who he was or why he was jailed. Many people believe the prisoner was the brother of King Louis XIV. He may have even been a twin brother. They think Louis XIV jailed him. With him jailed, no one could stop Louis from being the king.

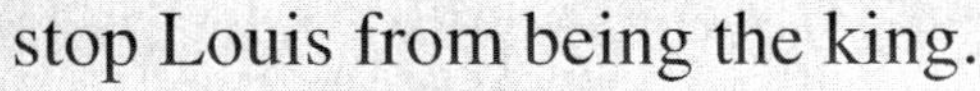

Vanishing Act

The Bermuda Triangle is a place where dozens of boats, planes, and people have vanished. It is located in the Atlantic Ocean. Some people think this area is very dangerous. They think there is a magnetic field there that causes compasses to stop working. Others think the strong water currents and bad weather are the reason for the danger.

In 1918, a U.S. Naval ship went missing. It had left the island of Barbados. It traveled into the Bermuda Triangle. The ship and crew of 306 people vanished without a trace. Some people blame storms or a wartime enemy. Others disagree with this theory. They say there would be remains of the ship or the crew if the disappearance had been due to a storm or wartime combat.

In 1945, five U.S. Navy bombers flew out of Florida on a training flight. The pilots became lost within the Bermuda Triangle. Through one of the plane's radios, the leader of the group said his compass was off. He said everything looked strange. He couldn't figure out where they were. Another plane was sent out to find them, it also vanished. The Navy called for all boats and planes in the area to look for them. But they were never found.

Anastasia

There was big trouble in Russia in the early 1900s. The people wanted to get rid of the old rulers. Nicholas II was the ruler at the time. He was married and had five children. Anastasia was his youngest daughter. On July 17, 1918, the secret police killed Nicholas and his family. But did Anastasia survive? For years, many people thought so. Several women claimed that each was the lost duchess. They each stepped forward to claim the family fortune. But in 2009, science proved them all wrong. It is certain that the whole family died that day.

Bigfoot

Many people in the Pacific Northwest claimed to have seen a giant, apelike, wild man. They say he roams through the forest. They claim he walks upright, is more than seven feet tall, and has huge feet. Some people have taken photos of an apelike man. But no one can tell for sure if it is a real creature or just a person in an ape suit! Some scientists think Bigfoot may be real.

Bigfoot is also called *Sasquatch*. This comes from a Salish Indian word meaning "wild man." Stories of wild men were told among the native people of the Pacific Northwest for centuries. J. W. Burns first wrote the stories down in the 1920s. He was the first to call the creature *Sasquatch*.

Think About It!

How are historians and detectives alike?

History's Mysteries

Masked Prisoner

From around 1669 until his death in 1703, a mysterious man was held in jails throughout France. Most of the time, he was in the Bastille. No one ever saw the man's face because it was always covered with a black velvet mask. The prisoner's name was Eustache Dauger, but that is probably not his real name. Dauger was told that if he talked about himself, he would be killed. Only the head of the Bastille was allowed to see his face. No one knows who he was or why he was jailed. Many people believe the prisoner was the brother of King Louis XIV—maybe even a twin brother. They think Louis XIV jailed him so no one could stop Louis from being the king.

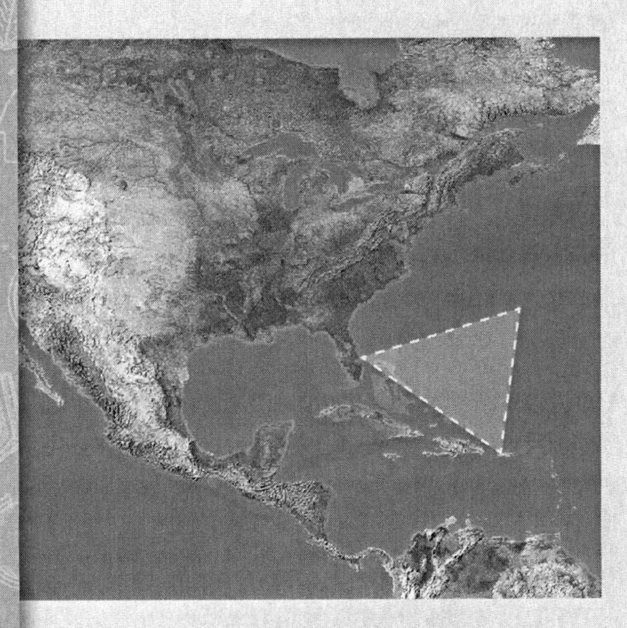

Vanishing Act

The Bermuda Triangle is a place where dozens of boats, planes, and people have vanished. It is located in the Atlantic Ocean. Some people think this area is very dangerous. They think there is a magnetic field there that causes compasses to stop working. Others think the strong water currents and weather conditions are the reason for the disappearances.

In 1918, a U.S. Naval ship went missing after leaving the island of Barbados and traveling into the Bermuda Triangle. The ship and crew of 306 people vanished without a trace. Some people blame storms or a wartime enemy; others say there would be remains of the ship or the crew if the disappearance had been due to a storm or wartime combat.

In 1945, five U.S. Navy bombers flew out of Fort Lauderdale, Florida, on a training flight. The pilots became lost within the Bermuda Triangle. Through one of the plane's radios, the leader of the group said his compass was off. He also said everything looked strange and he couldn't figure out where they were. A sixth plane that was sent out to find them also vanished. And, although the Navy called for all planes and boats in the area to look out for them, no trace of the planes was ever found.

Anastasia

There was big trouble in Russia in the early 1900s. The people wanted to get rid of the old rulers, and Nicholas II was the seated ruler at that time. He was married and had five children. Anastasia Romanov was his youngest daughter. On July 17, 1918, the secret police executed Nicholas and his family. But did Anastasia survive? For years, many people thought so. Several women claimed each was the lost duchess. They each stepped forward to claim the family fortune. But in 2009, science proved them all wrong. It is certain that the entire family died that day.

Bigfoot

Many people in the Pacific Northwest claimed to have seen a giant, apelike, wild man. They say he roams through the forest. They claim he walks upright, is more than seven feet tall, and has huge feet. Some people have taken photos of a giant, apelike creature, but no one can tell for sure if it is a real or just a person in an ape suit! Some scientists think Bigfoot may be real.

Bigfoot is also called *Sasquatch*, which comes from a Salish Indian word meaning "wild man." Stories of wild men were told among the native people of the Pacific Northwest for centuries. J. W. Burns, who first wrote the stories down in the 1920s, was the first to call the creature *Sasquatch*.

Think About It!

What strategies do historians and detectives use to solve mysteries?

Go-Kart Racing

Building a Machine

Many people enjoy go-karts as a hobby. They find that part of the fun is building the kart. Working with others makes it even more fun. Building go-karts requires working as a team.

It is important to have a plan before starting to build. This plan might be a blueprint of some kind. It shows what the finished kart will look like. Making a plan uses math skills. The builder must measure and estimate. Calculations need to be made. Using math lets drivers build the kart that's right for them.

A blueprint for building a go-kart shows all the parts needed to make it run. The frame of the kart is the first part to think about. The other parts can be changed later, but the frame can't be. The frame can come in different shapes. It can be designed to help the kart move at a faster pace.

The engine is another important part of a go-kart. It makes the kart move. The power of the engine affects how fast the kart can go. Brakes are also important. They make the kart stop. A plan for a go-kart may show tires, seats, and a steering wheel. Following a blueprint is helpful. It makes the building process go much more smoothly.

The builder uses tools to put the parts together. Young go-kart drivers must work with an adult when using power tools. These tools can be very dangerous. Safety goggles or gloves may be needed. Power saws and drills are often used to build a kart. A saw cuts the wood or metal for the frame. It can cut other parts for the kart, too. A drill makes holes for bolts. Then the parts can be joined together. No driver wants the kart to fall apart in the middle of a ride!

Full Throttle

The thrill of a go-kart comes from the speed of the ride. The engine and the wheels make the kart move forward. Some engines are electric. Others get energy from gasoline. But not all go-karts have engines. Some are pushed down a hill. Drivers let gravity take over to carry them down the hill.

A driver's heart races as the kart speeds around the course. Drivers train so they can stay calm. They need to be safe as they drive at top speeds. Different types of go-karts are built to travel safely at different speeds. Some go-karts are built for younger drivers. They can go about 20 miles (32 kilometers) per hour. Superkarts are special go-karts. They can go over 100 miles (161 kilometers) per hour. Superkarts are most often raced on large racetracks.

If go-karts are going to move so quickly, they need to be able to slow down as well! Luckily, brakes are standard on every go-kart. Braking is a good way to stop a go-kart. Without brakes, drivers would have to use their feet to stop the kart—ouch! Most go-karts have brake pedals. Drivers use their feet to push the pedal. This makes the kart stop. Some go-karts have a hand brake. These brakes work by pulling on a lever. Brakes should allow a kart to stop quickly and safely. They need to work well on different surfaces. They should be tested on wet or dry courses. Brake pads slow a kart by applying pressure and friction. Once the wheels stop turning, the kart also stops moving.

Think About It!

What steps are needed to make a go-kart?

Go-Kart Racing

Building a Machine

Many people enjoy go-karts as a hobby. They find that part of the fun is actually building the kart and that working with someone else makes it even better. Constructing go-karts requires a lot of cooperation.

Before starting to build, it is important to have a plan, which might be a blueprint of some kind. It shows what the finished kart will look like. Making a plan uses math skills because there are measurements, estimates, and calculations to make. Using math lets drivers build the kart that's right for them.

A plan for building a go-kart shows all the parts needed to make it run. The frame of the kart is the first part to consider. The other parts can be changed later, but the frame cannot be. The frame can come in different shapes. It can be designed to help the kart move at a faster pace.

The engine is another important part of a go-kart because it makes the kart move. The power of the engine affects how fast the kart can go. Brakes are important because they make the kart stop. A plan for a go-kart may show tires, seats, and a steering wheel, too. Following a good plan makes the building process go much more smoothly.

The builder uses tools to put the parts together. Young go-kart drivers must work with an adult whenever using power tools because these tools can be very dangerous. Safety goggles or gloves may be needed. Power saws and drills are often used to build a kart. A saw cuts the wood or metal for the frame and can cut other parts of the kart, too. A drill makes holes for bolts and joins the parts together. No go-kart driver wants the kart to fall apart in the middle of a ride!

Full Throttle

The thrill of a go-kart comes from the speed of the ride. The engine and the wheels make the kart move forward. Some engines get energy from electricity, while others get it from gasoline. But not all go-karts have engines. Some are pushed down a hill and drivers let gravity take over.

A driver's heart races as the kart speeds around the course. Drivers train so they can stay calm. They need to be safe as they drive at top speeds. Different types of go-karts are built to travel safely at different speeds. Most go-karts that young drivers build can go about 20 miles (32 kilometers) per hour. Superkarts are special go-karts designed to go over 100 miles (161 kilometers) per hour. Superkarts are most often raced on large racetracks.

If go-karts are going to move so quickly, they need to be able to slow down as well! Luckily, brakes are standard on every go-kart. Braking is a good way to stop a go-kart. Without brakes, drivers would have to use their feet to stop the kart—ouch! Most go-karts have brake pedals. Drivers use their feet to push the pedal and make the kart stop. Some go-karts have a hand brake. These brakes work by pulling on a lever. Brakes should allow a kart to stop quickly and safely. They need to work well on different surfaces. They should be tested in wet or dry conditions. Brake pads slow a vehicle by applying pressure and friction. Once the wheels stop turning, the vehicle also stops moving.

Think About It!

Why is it important to have a blueprint before building a go-kart?

Go-Kart Racing

Building a Machine

Many people enjoy go-karts as a hobby. They discover part of the satisfaction is constructing the kart and that working alongside someone else makes it even more fun. Assembling go-karts requires a lot of cooperation.

It is necessary to have a design, or blueprint, before beginning to build in order to show what the finished kart will look like. Creating a plan requires mathematics skills because there are measurements, estimates, and calculations to make. Using math allows drivers to build a kart that is appropriate for them.

A blueprint for building a go-kart will outline all the components needed to make it functional. The frame of the kart is the first part to consider because, while the other parts can be altered later, the frame cannot. The frame can come in different shapes and can be designed to help the kart move at a faster pace.

The engine is another important part of a go-kart because it allows the kart to travel. The power of the engine affects how fast the kart can go, and brakes are important because they make the kart stop. A plan for a go-kart may include tires, seats, and a steering wheel, too. Creating and following a good blueprint makes the building process go much more efficiently.

The builder uses tools to put the pieces together. Younger go-kart drivers must always work with an adult whenever using power tools because these tools can be very dangerous. Safety goggles or gloves may be required. Power saws and drills are often used during the construction process. A saw cuts the wood or metal materials for the frame and can cut other parts of the kart, too. A drill makes holes for bolts and joins the parts together. No go-kart driver wants the kart to fall apart in the middle of a ride!

Full Throttle

The excitement of a go-kart comes from the speediness of the ride. The engine and the wheels make the kart move forward. Some engines acquire energy from electricity, while others use gasoline. But not all go-karts have engines. Some are pushed down a hill, and gravity takes over to carry the drivers down.

A driver's heart races as the kart speeds around the course. Drivers train so they can stay composed and to learn how to stay safe as they drive at top speeds. Different types of go-karts are built to travel safely at different speeds. Most go-karts that young drivers build can go about 20 miles (32 kilometers) per hour. Special go-karts called *superkarts* are designed to go over 100 miles (161 kilometers) per hour. Superkarts are usually raced on large racetracks.

If go-karts are going to move so quickly, they need to be able to slow down as well! Luckily, brakes are customary on every kart. Braking is a good way to stop a go-kart. Without brakes, drivers would have to use their feet to stop the kart—ouch! Most go-karts have brake pedals. Drivers use their feet to push the pedal and make the kart stop. Some go-karts have a hand brake, which works by pulling on a lever. Brakes should allow a kart to stop quickly and safely. They need to work well on a variety of surfaces, so they should be tested in wet or dry environments. Brake pads slow a vehicle by applying pressure and friction. Once the wheels stop turning, the vehicle also stops moving.

Think About It!

If you were creating a go-kart blueprint, what are three things you would be sure to include?

Food Groups

High-Energy Grains

Your body uses glucose for energy. Most food does not have glucose in it. But your body can help, it can change some foods into glucose. Proteins and fats can turn into energy. This takes a long time. Carbohydrates are different. It's easy for your body to turn them into energy. Foods like bread, pasta, and rice have a lot of carbohydrates. They are made from grains. These are high-energy foods.

A Stronger You

Everyone needs protein. It helps us stay healthy. Proteins help your body so it can build, fix, and maintain itself. Muscles, skin, and other organs are made mostly of protein. Proteins are made of smaller amino acids. Your body needs 22 different amino acids to be healthy. It can make 13 on its own. But there are nine you need to get from food. Meat and milk have all nine. They are animal proteins. Many proteins that come from plants don't have amino acids. Vegetarians do not eat meat. They must eat a variety of foods to get all their amino acids. Luckily, you don't need to eat all of them at the same time. Your body will take what it needs from each meal. It will match up the nutrients later.

Fruit

Fruits are a special part of a plant. They protect seeds as they grow into new plants. Many fruits are juicy and sweet. They often have vitamins and minerals. Many fruits are a great source of fiber, too. Plants grow in many places. So certain fruits are liked in different countries. If you grew up in Southeast Asia, you might like rambutans. These are tough red fruits. They have spines on the outside. In India, jackfruit is common. It tastes a little like pineapple. In China, people love to eat lychee for dessert. They look a bit like small rambutans and are very sweet. In Mexico, many people eat mangos and papaya.

Vegetables

What do vegetables bring to the table? They are high in vitamins and minerals. Some, like broccoli, have good amounts of protein, too. Vegetables can have a lot of fiber. When you eat a lot of them, you can lower your risk for many diseases. Some cancers and eye problems happen less in people who eat a lot of vegetables.

Dairy

Dairy products include milk and things made from milk, like cheese and yogurt. These foods are one way to get calcium. Your body needs it. Calcium is a mineral. It makes up a large part of your bones and teeth. Some people don't get enough calcium. Their bones and teeth can grow weak. Whole milk has a lot of fat in it. It is meant to give baby cows what they need. But it has too much fat for most people. There is a better option! Choose dairy foods marked *low fat* or *nonfat*.

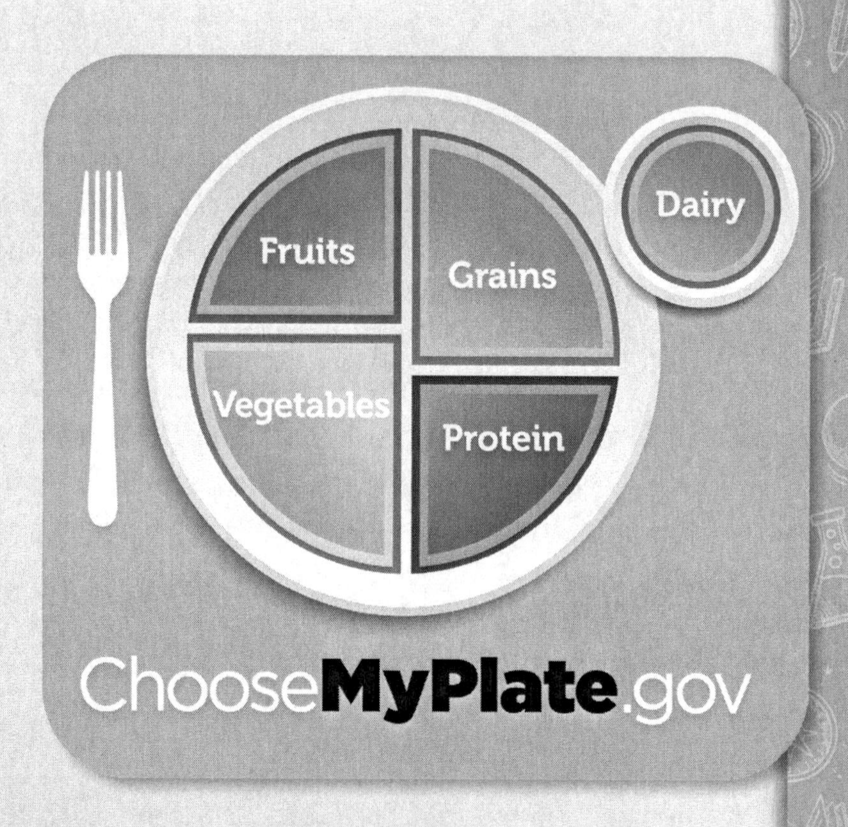

Think About It!

What are some reasons we should eat fruit, vegetables, and dairy?

Food Groups

High-Energy Grains

Your body uses glucose for energy. Most food doesn't have any glucose in it. But your body can change some foods into glucose. Proteins and fats can be changed into energy, but it takes a long time. It's easiest for your body to change carbohydrates into energy. Foods made from grains, such as bread, tortillas, and rice, have a lot of carbohydrates. These are high-energy foods.

A Stronger You

Everybody needs protein to stay healthy. Proteins help your body build, fix, and maintain itself. Muscles, skin, and other organs are made mostly of protein. Proteins are made of smaller amino acids. Your body needs 22 different amino acids to be healthy. It can make 13 of them on its own, but there are nine you need to get from your food. Animal proteins, like meat and milk, have all nine. But many proteins that come from plants don't. People who are vegetarians don't eat meat. They must eat a variety of foods to get all their amino acids. Luckily, you don't need to eat all of them at the same meal. Your body will take what it needs from each meal and match the nutrients up later.

Fruit

Fruits are a special part of a plant. They protect the seeds as they grow into new plants. Many fruits are juicy and sweet! They also usually have a lot of vitamins and minerals. And many fruits are a great source of fiber, too. Different plants grow in different places. So, different fruits are popular in different countries. If you grew up in Southeast Asia, you might like rambutans. These leathery red fruits have spines on the outside. In India, jackfruit is common. It tastes a little like pineapple. In China, people love to eat lychee for dessert. They look a bit like small rambutans and are very sweet. In Mexico, people like to eat mangos and papaya.

Vegetables

What do vegetables bring to the table? They are high in vitamins and minerals. Some, like broccoli, have good amounts of protein, too. Vegetables also usually have a lot of fiber. When you eat more vegetables, you can lower your risk for many serious diseases. Some cancers and eye problems tend to happen less in people who eat a lot of vegetables.

Dairy

Dairy products include milk and things made from milk, such as cheese and yogurt. These foods are one easy way to get the calcium your body needs. Calcium is a mineral that makes up a large part of your bones and teeth. If you don't get enough calcium, your bones and teeth can grow weak. Whole milk has a lot of fat in it. It is meant to give baby cows what they need. But it has too much fat for many people. For a healthier option, choose dairy foods marked *low fat* or *nonfat*.

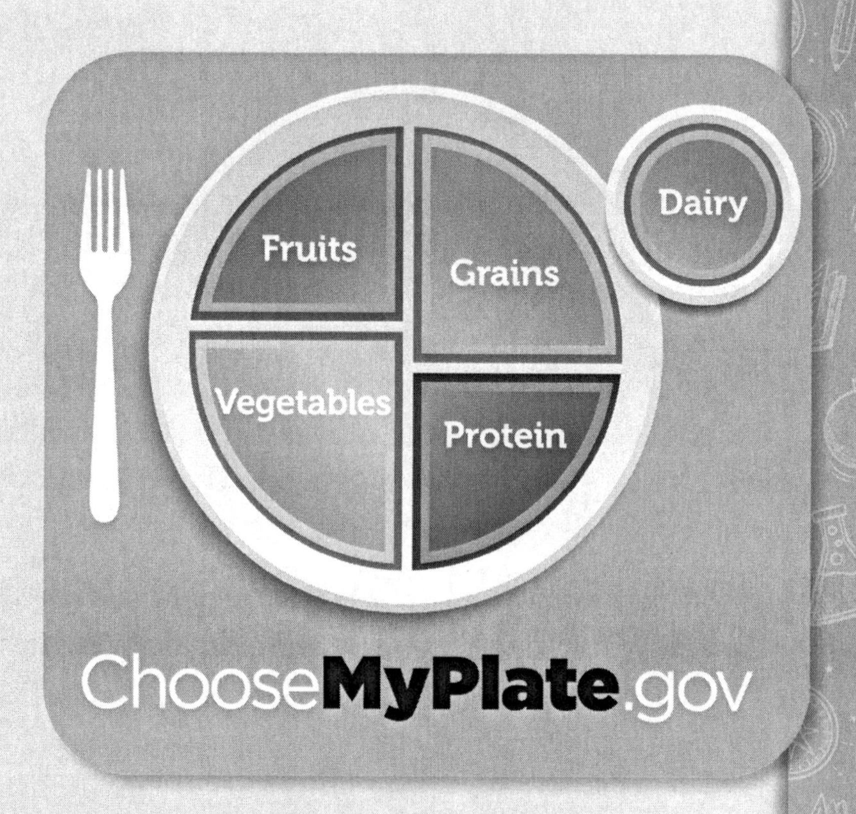

Think About It!

If you had to plan a meal, what might you include to make sure most of the food groups were included?

Food Groups

High-Energy Grains

Your body uses glucose for energy. Most food does not contain any glucose, but your body can transform some foods into glucose. Proteins and fats can be changed into energy, but it takes a long time. It's easiest for your body to change carbohydrates into energy. Foods made from grains, like bread, tortillas, and rice, have a lot of carbohydrates, so these are high-energy foods.

A Stronger You

Everybody requires protein to stay healthy because proteins help your body build, fix, and maintain itself. Muscles, skin, and other organs are made mostly of protein. Proteins are made of smaller amino acids, and your body needs 22 different ones to be healthy. It can make 13 of the amino acids on its own, but there are nine you need to get from your food. Animal proteins, like meat and milk, have all nine, but many proteins that come from plants do not. People who are vegetarians don't eat meat. They must eat a variety of foods to get all their amino acids. Luckily, you don't need to eat all of them at the same meal because your body will take what it needs from each meal and match up the nutrients later.

Fruit

Fruits are a special part of a plant that protects the seeds as they grow into new plants. Many fruits are juicy and sweet! They also usually have a lot of vitamins and minerals—many fruits are a great source of fiber, too. Different plants grow in different locations, so different fruits are popular in different countries. If you grew up in Southeast Asia, you might like rambutans, leathery red fruits that have spines on the outside. In India, jackfruit is common; it tastes a little like pineapple. In China, people love to eat lychee, which look a bit like small rambutans and are very sweet, for dessert. In Mexico, many people like to eat mangos and papaya.

Vegetables

What do vegetables bring to the table? They are high in vitamins and minerals, and some, like broccoli, even have good amounts of protein. Vegetables also usually have a lot of fiber. The more vegetables you eat, the lower your risk for many serious diseases. Some cancers and eye problems tend to happen less in people who eat a lot of vegetables.

Dairy

Dairy products include milk and things with milk as an ingredient, such as cheese and yogurt. These foods are one easy way to get the calcium your body needs. Calcium is a mineral that makes up a large part of your bones and teeth. If you don't get enough calcium, your bones and teeth can grow weak. Whole milk has a lot of fat in it. It is meant to give baby cows what they need, but it has too much fat for many people. For a healthier option, choose dairy foods marked *low fat* or *nonfat*.

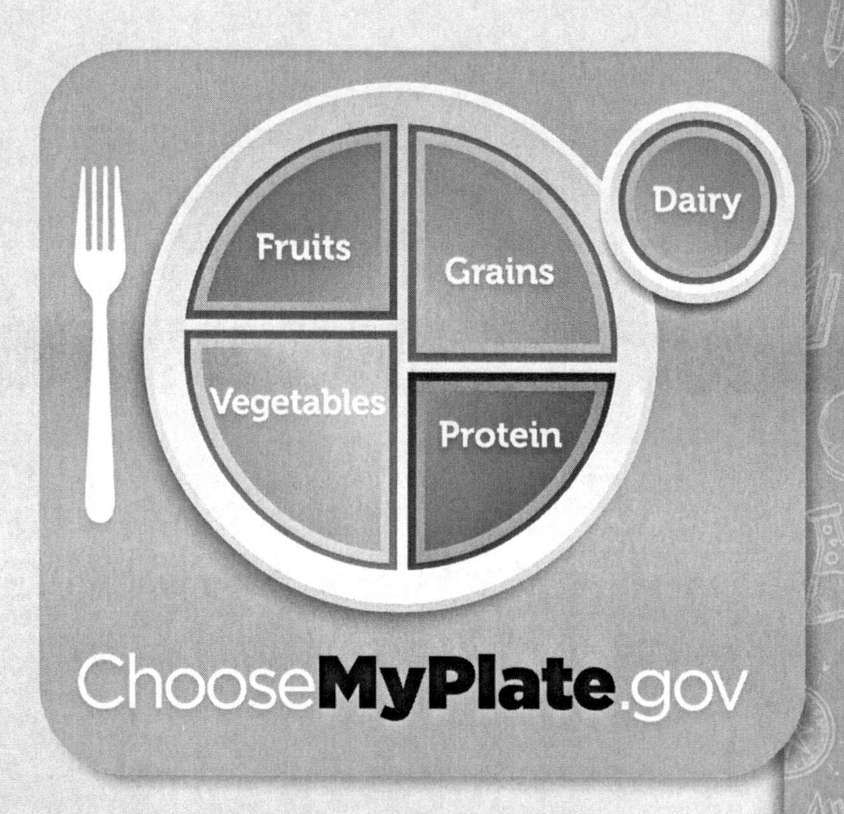

Think About It!

Some people say it's important to have a balanced meal. What does this mean? Do you think it is important? Explain your answer.

Eco-Predictions

Where Are the Fish?

Claymont Fishing Club members are worried. They look at the results of their yearly fishing contest. Where have all the fish gone? The people are troubled about Claymont Stream's ecosystem. The fishing club studies the stream's food chain. They want to see how fewer fish might change the life of the stream.

Call in the Expert

The mayor of Claymont calls Mei Chan to help. Ms. Chan is a park ranger. She studies a map of the stream. She wants to see what might be causing the problems. Then she predicts some reasons for the drop in the number of fish. She makes a diagram of her predictions. Ms. Chan will collect data on Claymont Stream's ecosystem. This will help her find answers.

Collecting Data

First, Ms. Chan tests the stream's water temperature. She does this every day for a week. Then, she tests the water temperature of three nearby streams. She makes a table of her data. She compares the results. They are almost the same. So she concludes that water temperature is not the problem.

Next, Ms. Chan tests the stream's water. She wants to see how much soil is in it. The water is clear. So dust from the paper mill is not the reason why fewer fish are in the stream. Then, Ms. Chan tests how clean the water is. The results are normal for a stream. Pollution does not seem to be a problem. Ms. Chan also collects data on the animal life in the stream. She swims in part of the stream. She counts any fish or frogs that she sees. Then, Ms. Chan uses a net to catch tadpoles. She counts them and puts them back. She also studies insects at the stream.

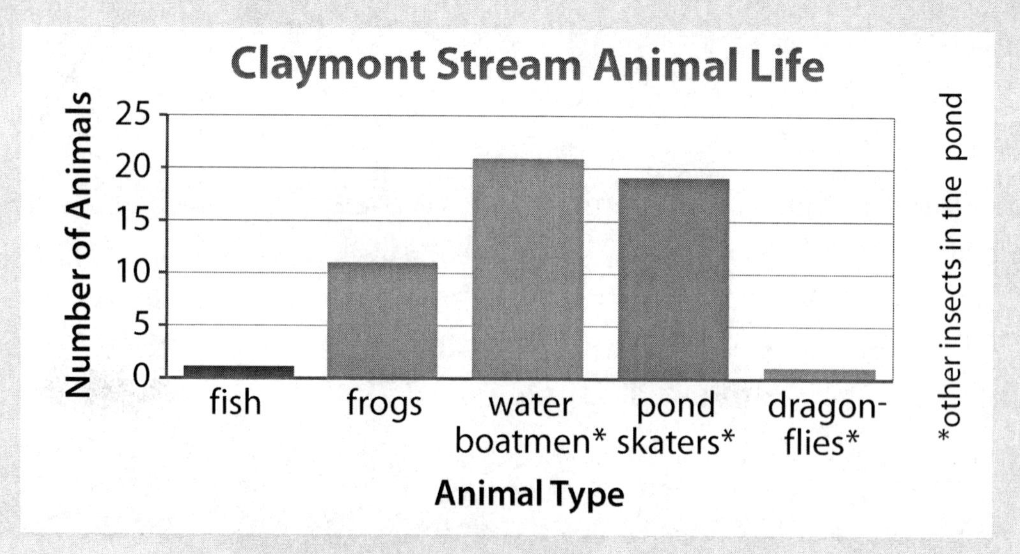

Ms. Chan puts her data in a table. She records all her animal studies on a bar graph. Claymont Stream has a lot of water insects. Frog numbers are also high. There are not enough fish to eat tadpoles and insects. But dragonfly numbers are going down. This is because frogs eat them. There are more frogs. So there are fewer dragonflies.

Ms. Chan collects data on the plants in the stream. Plants grow quickly in Claymont Stream. There are few fish to feed on them. Ms. Chan predicts that the plants will clog the stream. This may cause flooding in the future.

Predictions Can Become Solutions

Ms. Chan reviews her prediction diagram. She looks over her data. Water temperature is not a problem. There is no pollution from animal waste or mills. And the water is clear of soil and mud. Ms. Chan concludes that the problem is too much fishing. People catch too many fish from Claymont Stream. Ms. Chan tells the Claymont Fishing Club to ban fishing for three years. After that, people can fish. But they should only catch smaller amounts of fish. She also says that some stream plants should be taken out. This will keep the stream flowing properly.

Think About It!

What steps did Ms. Chan follow before making her final conclusion? What was her conclusion?

Eco-Predictions

Where Are the Fish?

Claymont Fishing Club members look at the results of their yearly fishing contest because they are worried. Where have all the fish gone? The people of Claymont are worried about Claymont Stream's ecosystem. The fishing club studies the food chain of the stream's ecosystem to see how fewer fish might change the life of the stream.

Call in the Expert

The mayor of Claymont calls Mei Chan, a park ranger, to help. She studies a map of the stream to see what might be causing the problems and predicts some reasons for the drop in the number of fish. She makes a diagram of her predictions. Ms. Chan will collect data on Claymont Stream and its ecosystem. This will help her find answers.

Collecting Data

First, Ms. Chan tests the stream's water temperature every day for a week. Then she tests the water temperature of three nearby streams. She makes a table of her data and compares the results. The water temperatures are almost the same, so she concludes that water temperature is not causing the problem.

Then, Ms. Chan tests Claymont Stream's water to see how much soil is in it; the water is clear. So the paper mill is not the reason why fewer fish are in the stream. Next, Ms. Chan tests how clean the water is, and the results are normal for a stream. Pollution does not seem to be a problem. Ms. Chan also collects data on the animal life in the stream. She swims in a part of the stream and counts any fish or frogs she sees. Then, Ms. Chan uses a net to catch tadpoles, counts them, and puts them back. Ms. Chan also studies insects at the stream.

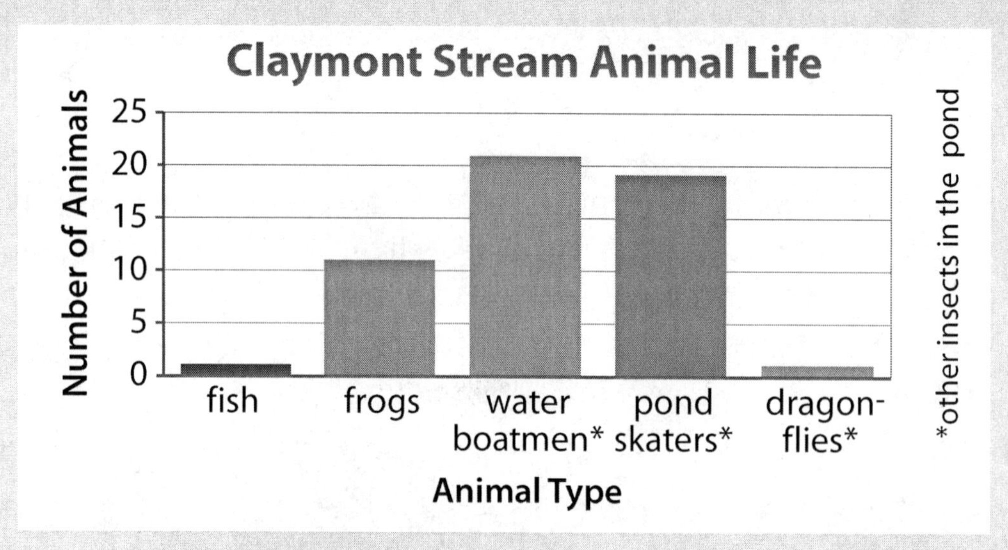

She puts her data in a table. Ms. Chan records all her animal studies on a bar graph. Claymont Stream has many water insects, and frog numbers are also high. There are not enough fish to eat tadpoles and insects. But dragonfly numbers are decreasing because frogs eat dragonflies. When there are more frogs, there are fewer dragonflies.

Ms. Chan collects data on the plants in the stream. Plants grow rapidly in Claymont Stream because there are few fish to feed on them. Ms. Chan predicts that the plants will congest the stream, which may cause flooding in the future.

Predictions Can Become Solutions

Ms. Chan reviews her prediction diagram and looks over her data. Water temperature is not a problem for the stream. There is no pollution from animal waste or factories. And the water is clear of soil and mud. So Ms. Chan concludes that the problem is over-fishing. People catch too many fish from Claymont Stream. Ms. Chan tells the Claymont Fishing Club to ban fishing for three years. After that, people should only catch smaller amounts of fish. She also says that some stream plants should be taken out. This will keep the stream flowing properly.

Think About It!

How will a ban help with the lack of fish at Claymont Stream?

Eco-Predictions

Where Are the Fish?

Claymont Fishing Club members look at the results of their yearly fishing competition because they are concerned. Why have so many fish disappeared? The people of Claymont are worried about Claymont Stream's ecosystem. The fishing club studies the food chain of the stream's ecosystem to see how fewer fish could possibly alter the life of the stream.

Call in the Expert

The mayor of Claymont contacts Mei Chan, a park ranger, to help. Ms. Chan studies a map of the stream to see what might be causing the problems and predicts some possibilities to explain the drop in the fish population. She creates a diagram of her predictions and will collect information on Claymont Stream and the stream's ecosystem. This will help her discover answers.

Collecting Data

First, Ms. Chan tests the stream's water temperature every day for a week; then she tests the water temperature of three nearby streams. She generates a table of her data and compares the results. The water temperatures are almost identical, so she concludes that water temperature is not causing the problem.

Then Ms. Chan tests Claymont Stream's water to see how much soil is in it, but the water is clear. She concludes that the paper mill is not the reason why fewer fish are in the stream. Next, Ms. Chan tests the cleanliness of the water, and the results are typical for a stream. Pollution does not seem to be a problem. Ms. Chan also collects data on the animal life in the stream. She swims in a section of the stream and counts any fish or frogs she observes. Then she uses a net to catch tadpoles, counts them, and puts them back. Ms. Chan also studies insects at the stream.

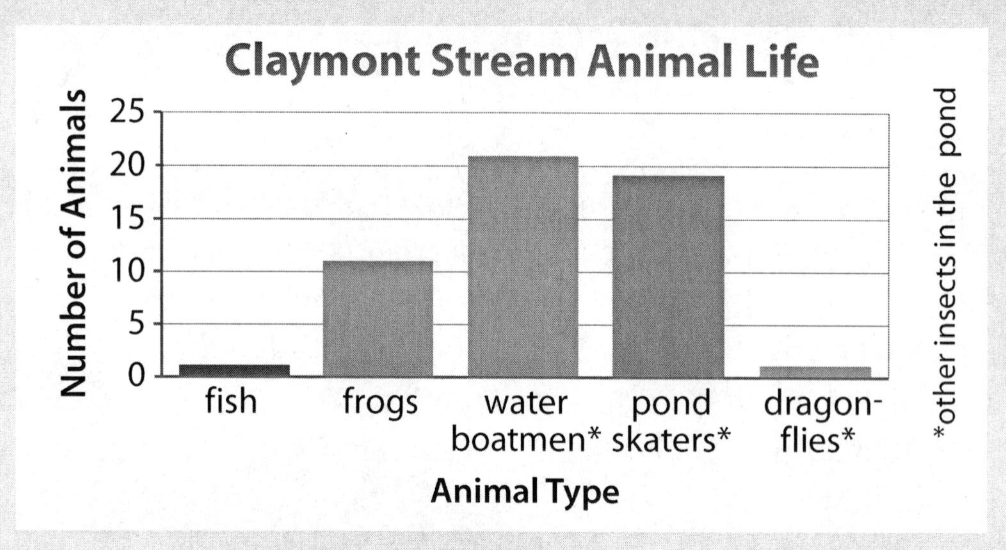

She puts her data in a table and records all her animal studies on a bar graph. Claymont Stream has many water insects, and the frog population is also high. There are not enough fish to eat tadpoles and insects. But dragonfly numbers are decreasing because frogs eat dragonflies. When there are higher numbers of frogs, there are fewer dragonflies.

Ms. Chan collects data on the plants in the stream and learns that plants grow rapidly in Claymont Stream because there are few fish to feed on them. Ms. Chan predicts that the plants will congest the stream, which could possibly cause flooding in the future.

Predictions Can Become Solutions

Ms. Chan reviews her prediction diagram and looks over her data. Water temperature is not a problem for the stream; there is no pollution from animal waste or factories; the water is clear of soil and mud. So, Ms. Chan concludes that the problem is over-fishing. People catch too many fish from Claymont Stream. Ms. Chan tells the Claymont Fishing Club to ban fishing for three years, and after that, allow people to only catch smaller numbers of fish. She also advises that some stream plants should be taken out, which will keep the stream flowing properly.

Think About It!

What other solutions could Ms. Chan propose to the Claymont Fishing Club?

Journeys: Land, Air, Sea

Land

Many people use street maps at work. Movers carry goods. Taxi drivers take people to places. Ambulance drivers take people to hospitals. Street maps help these people find the best routes to take.

Street maps have lines on them. They are horizontal and vertical. These lines cross. They form a grid of cells. Each cell has a letter and a number. This letter and number is called a *grid coordinate*. These help people find places. What will you find at the grid coordinate C2? First, find the letter *C*, and then find the number 2. Now, find the cell where these coordinates cross. You find Central Park.

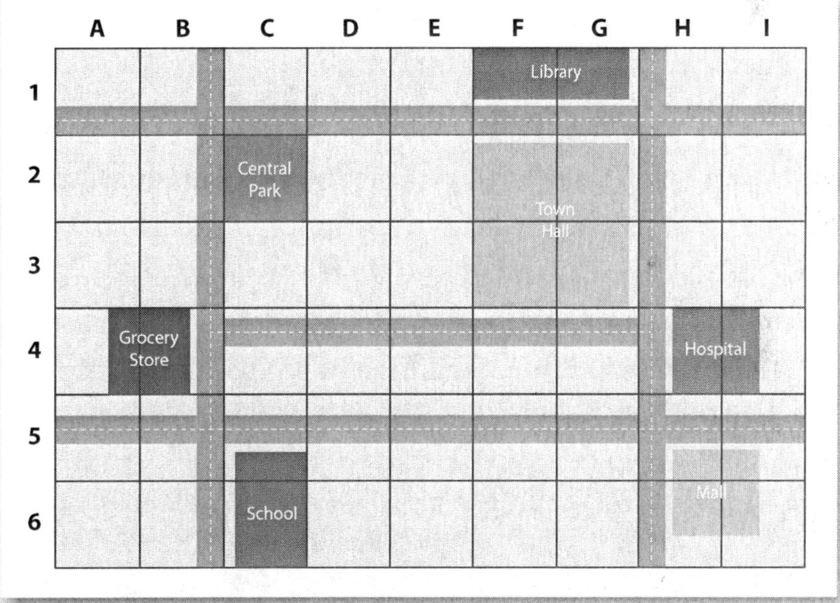

Road maps may show larger areas than street maps. Like street maps, road maps have a grid. Road maps also have keys. The key shows symbols. Each symbol stands for something on the map. Truck drivers use road maps to plan their trips. They use a map's scale to work out a distance. A map's scale is written as a ratio. A ratio compares two numbers. So on a map, the scale may be 1:20. This means that 1 inch (2.5 centimeters) equals 20 miles (32 kilometers) of distance.

Some people use a global positioning system (GPS). They may have them in their trucks or cars. A GPS uses satellites that rotate around the Earth. The satellites send signals to GPS receivers. A GPS can show location, speed, and direction. A GPS can also show street maps. The street maps show the route to an address. They also show which way the car is going. As the car moves, the map changes. It shows the new location.

Air

Airplane pilots use maps, too. They use them to work out their flight routes. These maps are called *air charts*. These charts show the main landmarks on the ground. Some air charts cover very large areas. Like street and road maps, air charts are drawn to scale.

Today, nearly every airplane has a GPS. The GPS helps the pilot see where the plane is. It also shows how high the plane is flying. And the GPS can show distance between places.

Sea

People who sail ships and boats also use maps. These maps are called *sea charts*. Like other maps, sea charts have keys. They also have compass roses. A compass rose is an illustrated compass in a circle. Sea charts show how deep the water is, too. They show islands and lighthouses. Some sea charts even show harbors and bridges.

Ships also use GPS. A GPS can be used anywhere in the world. The GPS can tell a captain where a ship is. The captain can also use the GPS to work out the distance and directions to a destination. Most ships and boats also have a compass. Just like a compass on land and in the air, a sea compass shows direction. The points on the compass help the crew figure out in which direction the ships or boats are sailing.

Think About It!

What are some ways maps help with various forms of transportation?

Journeys: Land, Air, Sea

Land

Many people use street maps at work. Couriers carry goods, taxi drivers take people to places, and ambulance drivers take people to hospitals. Street maps help these people find the best routes to take.

Street maps have horizontal and vertical lines on them, which cross and form a grid of cells. Each cell has a letter and a number. This letter and number is called a *grid coordinate*. Grid coordinates help people find locations. What will you locate at the grid coordinate C2? First, locate the letter *C*, and then locate the number 2. Now, locate the cell where these coordinates cross. You find Central Park.

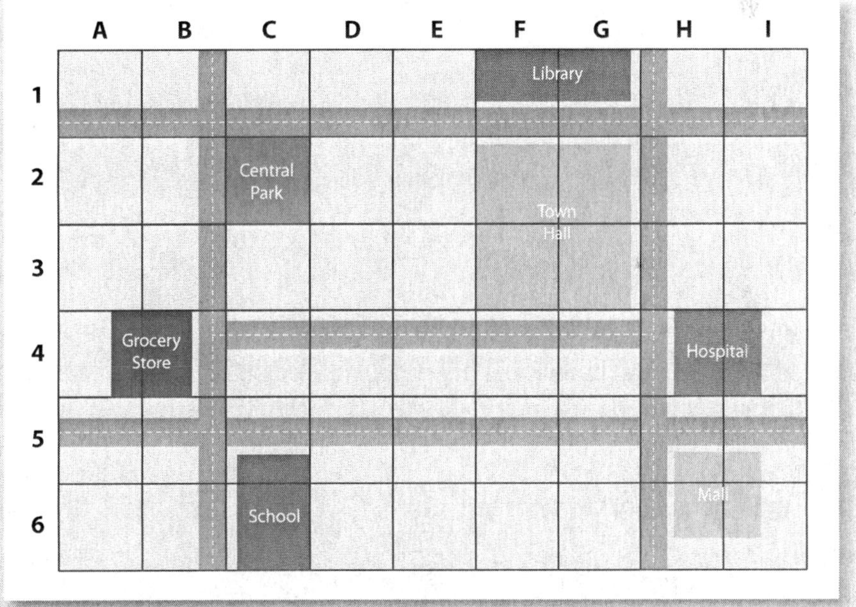

Road maps may show larger areas than street maps. Like street maps, road maps have grid coordinates, but road maps also have keys. The key shows the symbols on a map and what each symbol stands for. Truck drivers use road maps to plan their trips. They use a map's scale to work out distances. A map's scale is written as a ratio. A ratio is a comparison of two numbers. So on a map, the scale may be 1:20. This means that 1 inch (2.5 centimeters) equals 20 miles (32 kilometers) of distance.

Some people use a global positioning system (GPS) in their trucks or cars. A GPS uses satellites that orbit Earth, the satellites send signals to GPS receivers. A GPS can show location, speed, and direction. A GPS shows street maps. The street maps show the route to a location and the direction the car is going. As the car moves, the map changes to show its new location.

Air

Airplane pilots use maps to work out their flight routes. These maps are called *air charts*, and they show the main landmarks on the ground. Some air charts cover very large areas. Similar to street and road maps, air charts are drawn to scale.

Today, nearly every airplane has a GPS. The GPS helps the pilot see where the plane is and how high it is flying. The GPS can also show distance between locations.

Sea

People who sail ships and boats also use maps, called *sea charts*. Like other maps, sea charts have keys. They also have compass roses that are illustrated compasses drawn in circles. Sea charts also show how deep the water is. They show islands and lighthouses. Some sea charts show harbors and bridges, too.

Ships also use GPS. A GPS can be used anywhere in the world. The GPS can tell a captain the ship's location. The captain can also use the GPS to work out the distance and directions to a destination. Most ships and boats also have compasses. Just like compasses on land and in the air, sea compasses also show direction. The points on the compasses help the crew figure out which direction the ships or boats are sailing.

Think About It!

Why are maps important for land, air, and sea transportation?

Journeys: Land, Air, Sea

Land

Many people use street maps in their careers. Couriers deliver merchandise, taxi drivers transport people to their intended locations, and ambulance drivers whisk the sick and injured to hospitals. Street maps help these people find the most efficient routes to take.

Street maps have horizontal and vertical lines, which intersect and form a grid of cells. Each cell has a letter and a number; this letter and number is called a *grid coordinate*. Grid coordinates help people find locations. What will you locate at the grid coordinate C2? First, locate the letter *C*, and then find the number 2. Now, locate the cell where these coordinates cross. You find Central Park.

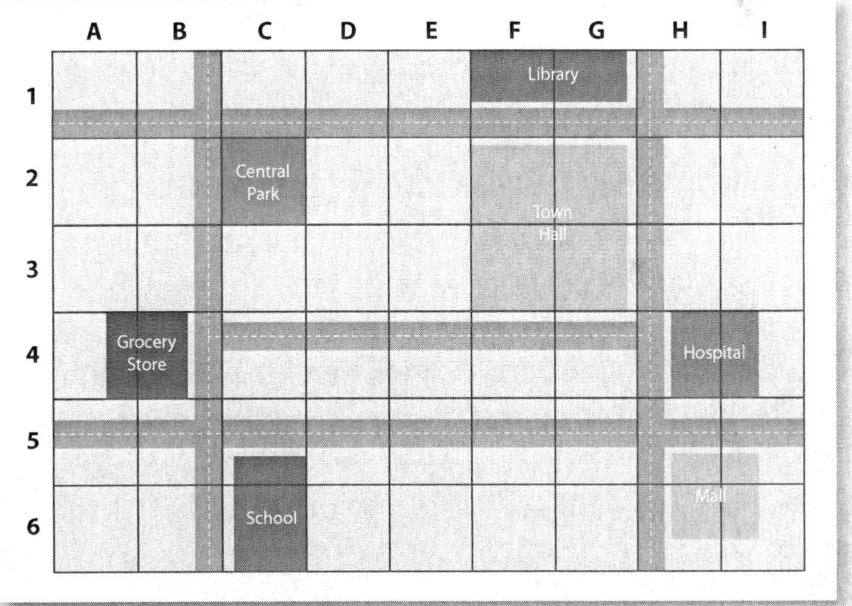

Road maps may show larger areas than street maps. Similar to street maps, road maps have grid coordinates, but road maps also have keys. The key shows symbols and what each symbol represents on the map. Truck drivers use road maps to organize their trips. They use a map's scale, written as a ratio, to work out distances. A ratio is a comparison of two numbers. So on a map, the scale may be 1:20, which means that 1 inch (2.5 centimeters) equals 20 miles (32 kilometers) of distance.

Some people use a global positioning system (GPS) in their trucks or vehicles. A GPS uses satellites that orbit Earth, and the satellites send signals to GPS receivers. A GPS can show location, speed, and direction, as well as street maps. The street maps show the route to a location and the direction the vehicle is going. As the car moves, the map changes to show its new location.

Air

Airplane pilots use maps to figure out their flight routes. These maps are called *air charts*, and they show the major landmarks on the ground. Some air charts cover an immense expanse of land. Similar to street and road maps, air charts are created to scale.

Today, nearly every airplane has a GPS. The GPS assists the pilot to see where the plane is, how high it is flying, and to show the distance between locations.

Sea

People who sail ships and boats also use maps, called *sea charts*. Like other maps, sea charts have keys, and they also have compass roses that are illustrated compasses drawn in circles. Sea charts show how deep the water is and the locations of islands and lighthouses. Some sea charts show harbors and bridges, too.

Ships also use GPS, which can be used anywhere in the world. The GPS can convey the ship's location to a captain. The captain can also use the GPS to figure out the distance and directions to a particular destination. Most ships and boats also have compasses, and just like compasses on land and in the air, sea compasses indicate direction. The points on the compasses help the crew determine in which direction the ships or boats are sailing.

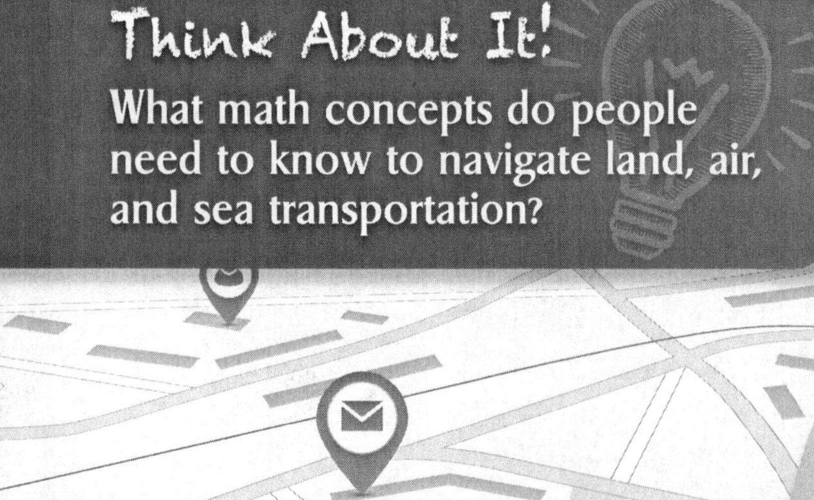

Patterns Around Us

Patterns in Nature

There are many patterns in nature. Plants are known by their leaf shapes and by the veins on their leaves. Look at some leaves. The patterns vary for each kind of tree. Even flower petals are in patterns. Daisies have long, narrow petals. They form circles.

Many animals have patterns on their bodies. Bees have striped patterns. Butterflies and moths have patterns on their wings. Leopards have spotted patterns. Their spots are used as camouflage in the long grass. Zebras have black and white stripes. Zebras can recognize one another. The striped patterns are unique for each animal!

Rocks often show patterns. Layers of rock build up. It takes millions of years. These layers are called *strata*. The strata make a pattern. It can be seen on cliff faces. The Grand Canyon is in Arizona. You can see many layers of strata there. Each layer of rock is its own color. The layers form striped patterns on the cliff faces. Experts study these patterns. Some layers show that the area was once a shallow sea. Other layers show that the area was a swamp or a desert.

Geometric Patterns

Geometric patterns are easy to make. You can repeat one shape to make a simple pattern. If you change the colors, the pattern will look different. Try making a pattern with shapes. When the shapes are turned or flipped the pattern changes. This is called a *transformation*. Transforming a shape will make a complex pattern. Turning, or rotating, a shape makes another pattern.

People use tiles. They can make patterns. They have done this for thousands of years. The patterns are called *tessellations*. These patterns cover spaces. There are no overlaps or gaps by the shapes. Only a few shapes are used for these patterns. Squares, triangles, and hexagons are used. These shapes fit neatly together. So they work for tessellations. Circles will not fit this pattern. They will need other shapes added to fill the gaps. Sometimes, the patterns are inside a shape, such as a square. This is repeated over and over. Other tessellations use symmetry.

Number Patterns

We have a system of numbers. It is based on patterns. They are in groups of 10. We count from 1 to 10. Then we repeat the numbers. There are more sets of 10. Then there are sets of 100. Then there are sets of 1,000. If we keep counting this pattern goes on and on. The same pattern of numbers keeps coming. We can see many patterns in a grid of 100 numbers. If we can count by 10s. Then we get a vertical pattern. When we count by 9s, we get a diagonal pattern.

Numbers make many patterns. It is easy to multiply by 9s. You just need to know there is a pattern. Think of the number in the tens column. It is always 1 less than the number you are multiplying by. And the sum of the numbers always adds up to 9.

Think About It!

What patterns do you see in your natural world?

Patterns Around Us

Patterns in Nature

There are many patterns in nature. Plants are known by their leaf shapes and by the vein patterns on their leaves. Look at some leaves. The patterns are different for each kind of tree. Even flower petals are in patterns. Daisies have long, narrow petals that form circles.

Many animals have patterns on their bodies. Bees have striped patterns. Butterflies and moths have patterns on their wings. Leopards have spotted patterns. Their spots are used as camouflage in the long grass. Zebras have black and white stripes. Zebras can recognize one another. The striped patterns are different on each animal!

Rocks often show patterns. Layers of rock build up over millions of years. These layers are called *strata*. The pattern of the different strata can be seen on cliff faces. At the Grand Canyon in Arizona, you can see many layers of strata. Each layer of rock is its own color. The layers form striped patterns on the cliff faces. Scientists study these patterns. Some layers show that the area was once a shallow sea. Other layers show that the area was a swamp or a desert.

Geometric Patterns

Geometric patterns are easy to make. Repeating just one shape makes a simple pattern. You can make the pattern look different by changing colors. You can also use different shapes. You can even change the positions of the shapes by flipping or turning them. This is called *transformation*. Transforming a shape, such as turning or flipping it, makes a more complex pattern. Turning, or rotating, a shape makes another pattern.

tessellation

People have used tiles to make patterns for thousands of years. These patterns are called *tessellations*. A tessellation is a pattern that covers a space. There are no overlaps or gaps between the shapes. Polygons are used for these types of patterns. Squares, triangles, and hexagons fit neatly together by themselves in tessellations. Circles will not fit the pattern unless other shapes are added to fill the gaps. In some tessellations, the patterns are inside a shape, such as a square. This is repeated over and over again. Other tessellations have symmetrical patterns.

Number Patterns

Our system of numbers is based on patterns in groups of 10. We count from 1 to 10 and then repeat the numbers in more sets of 10. Then we count in sets of 100, then sets of 1,000, and so on. No matter how far we count, the same pattern of numbers keeps going. We can see many patterns in a grid of 100 numbers. If we count by 10s, we get a vertical pattern on the grid. Counting by 9s makes a diagonal pattern.

Numbers make many patterns. It is easy to multiply by 9s if you know there is a pattern. The number in the tens column is always 1 less than the number you are multiplying by. And the sum of the numbers always adds up to 9.

Think About It!

Look around and make a list of patterns you see. Describe each pattern specifically.

Patterns Around Us

Patterns in Nature

There are many patterns in the environment. Plants can be recognized by the shapes of their leaves and by the vein patterns on their leaves. If you study some leaves you will see the patterns are different for each species of tree. Even flower petals are in patterns. Daisies have long, narrow petals that form circles.

Many animals have patterns on their bodies. Bees have striped patterns, and butterflies and moths have patterns on their wings. Leopards have spotted patterns—their spots are used as camouflage in the long grass. Zebras have black and white stripes. Zebras can recognize one another because the striped patterns are different on each animal!

Rocks frequently display patterns. Layers of rock, called *strata,* build up over millions of years. The pattern of the different strata can be seen on cliff faces. At the Grand Canyon in Arizona, you can see numerous layers of strata. Each layer of rock is a different color, and the layers form striped patterns on the cliff faces. Scientists study these patterns. Some layers show that the area was once a shallow sea, while other layers show that the area was a swamp or a desert.

Geometric Patterns

Geometric patterns are easy to make. Repeating just one shape makes a simple pattern. You can make the pattern look different by changing colors, or you can use different shapes. You can even change the positions of the shapes by flipping or turning them, which is called *transformation.* Transforming a shape, such as turning or flipping it, makes a more complex pattern. Turning, or rotating, a shape makes another pattern.

tessellation

People have used tiles to make patterns for thousands of years. These patterns, called *tessellations*, are patterns that cover a space with no overlaps or gaps between the shapes. Only certain polygons are used for these types of patterns. Squares, triangles, and hexagons fit neatly together by themselves in tessellations. Circles are unable to fit the pattern unless other shapes are added to fill the gaps. In some tessellations, the patterns are inside a shape, such as a square. This is repeated over and over again. Other tessellations have symmetrical patterns.

Number Patterns

Our system of numbers is based on patterns in groups of 10. We count from 1 to 10 and then repeat the numbers in more sets of 10, then in sets of 100, then sets of 1,000, and so on. No matter how far we count, the same pattern of numbers keeps appearing. We can see various patterns in a grid of 100 numbers. If we count by 10s, we get a vertical pattern on the grid. Counting by 9s makes a diagonal pattern, moving from right to left.

Numbers make many patterns. It is easy to multiply by 9s if you know there is a pattern. The number in the tens column is always 1 less than the number you are multiplying by, and the sum of the numbers always adds up to 9.

Think About It!

Create a complex number pattern of your own. Explain the pattern in words.

All About Sharks

Ancient Sharks

Different sharks have lived in the ocean for almost 400 million years. The megalodon shark lived 1.6 to 16 million years ago. It grew up to 50 feet (15 meters) in length. Its jaws were 6.5 feet (2 meters) wide. Its teeth could be up to 8 inches (20 centimeters) long. It weighed around 20 tons (18,144 kilograms). This is as much as five elephants weigh. A megalodon shark was around three times the length of a great white shark.

Dorsal Fins

Shark	Height of Dorsal Fin
dwarf dogfish	2.5 cm
cookie-cutter shark	3.75 cm
angel shark	10 cm
bullhead shark	20 cm
thresher shark	33 cm
Greenland shark	50 cm
basking shark	100 cm
great white shark	100 cm
whale shark	228 cm

Shark Parts

Today, more than half of all shark species are less than 3 feet (1 meter) long. But some grow much larger. And they have unusual features. The hammerhead shark has eyes on the ends of its head. It swings its head from side to side to see. Its head can grow up to half as long as its body. Thresher sharks use their tails to slap and slash other fish. This makes it easy to catch and eat their prey. Their tails can grow as long as their bodies.

Sharks often lose their teeth when they are catching their prey. So they are always growing new teeth. Sharks can have up to 3,000 teeth at a time. Shark teeth often grow in rows of five. A shark can go through 30,000 teeth in a lifetime!

The fin on top of a shark's back is called the *dorsal fin*. It is this fin that can often be seen above the water. Dorsal fins are stiff. A shark's fins help it stay upright in the water. All sharks have one or two dorsal fins.

Types of Sharks

The whale shark is the biggest fish in the world. It grows to more than 40 feet (12 meters) long. It can weigh up to 13 tons (about 11,793 kilograms). Whale sharks are slow swimmers. They have a top speed of 3 miles per hour (5 kilometers per hour). Whale sharks swim with their mouths open. They suck in water. The water is filled with plankton and small fish. Whale sharks' mouths can be 5 feet (1.5 meters) wide. They can suck in over 1,500 gallons (5,678 liters) of water an hour.

The great white shark is one of the most famous types of shark. Movies have even been made about them! Most great white sharks grow between 12 and 20 feet (about 3.5 to 6 meters) long. That's about as long as a van. Great white sharks are amazing hunters. They can reach speeds of 25 miles per hour (40 kilometers per hour). They can leap out of the water to catch their prey.

The swell shark sucks water in when it is scared. It can blow itself up to three times its normal size. It can wedge itself between rocks. That means no predators can get it out.

A cookie-cutter shark has long, sharp teeth. It bites and holds on to bigger prey. When it lets go, the bite looks like a cookie shape.

Shark Measurements

Shark	Average length	Average weight
dwarf dogfish	6 inches (15 cm)	1.5 ounces (43 g)
cookie-cutter shark	20 inches (50 cm)	5.5 ounces (156 g)
bullhead shark	40 inches (1 m)	20 pounds (9 kg)
angel shark	5 feet (1.5 m)	66 pounds (30 kg)
thresher shark	15 feet (4.5 m)	350 pounds (159 kg)
Greenland shark	20 feet (6 m)	2,200 pounds (998 kg)
great white shark	20 feet (6 m)	7,000 pounds (3,200 kg)
basking shark	33 feet (10 m)	15,400 pounds (6,985 kg)
whale shark	40 feet (12 m)	28,700 pounds (13,018 kg)

Think About It!

What are three things you learned about sharks from this passage?

All About Sharks

Ancient Sharks

Different sharks have lived in the ocean for almost 400 million years. The megalodon shark lived 1.6 to 16 million years ago. The megalodon measured up to 50 feet (15 meters) in length. Its jaws were 6.5 feet (2 meters) wide, and its teeth were up to 8 inches (20 centimeters) long. It weighed around 20 tons (18,144 kilograms), which is as much as five elephants. A megalodon shark was around three times the length of a great white shark.

Dorsal Fins

Shark	Height of Dorsal Fin
dwarf dogfish	2.5 cm
cookie-cutter shark	3.75 cm
angel shark	10 cm
bullhead shark	20 cm
thresher shark	33 cm
Greenland shark	50 cm
basking shark	100 cm
great white shark	100 cm
whale shark	228 cm

Shark Parts

Today, more than half of all shark species are less than 3 feet (1 meter) long, but some species grow much larger and have unusual features. The hammerhead shark has eyes on the ends of its head and swings its head from side to side to see. Its head can grow up to half as long as its body. Thresher sharks use their tails to slap and slash other fish, which makes their prey easier to catch and eat. Their tails can grow as long as their bodies.

Sharks often lose their teeth when they are catching their prey, so they are always growing new teeth. Sharks can have up to 3,000 teeth at a time. Shark teeth often grow in rows of five. A shark can go through 30,000 teeth in a lifetime!

The fin on top of a shark's back is called the *dorsal fin*. It is this fin that can often be seen above the water. Dorsal fins are stiff and help the shark stay upright in the water. All sharks have one or two dorsal fins.

Types of Sharks

The whale shark is the biggest fish in the world. It grows more than 40 feet (12 meters) long and can weigh up to 13 tons (about 11,793 kilograms). Whale sharks are slow swimmers with a top speed of only 3 miles per hour (5 kilometers per hour). Whale sharks swim with their mouths open. They suck in water that is filled with plankton and small fish. Whale sharks' mouths can be 5 feet (1.5 meters) wide and can suck in over 1,500 gallons (5,678 liters) of water an hour.

Great white sharks are one of the most famous species of shark. Movies have even been made about them! Most great white sharks grow between 12 and 20 feet (about 3.5 to 6 meters) long. That's about as long as a van. Great white sharks are amazing hunters. They can reach speeds of 25 miles per hour (40 kilometers per hour) and can leap out of the water to catch their prey.

The swell shark sucks water in when it gets scared. It can blow itself up to three times its normal size. It can wedge itself between rocks so no predator can reach it.

A cookie-cutter shark has long, sharp teeth and is able to bite and hold on to bigger prey. When it lets go, the bite resembles a cookie shape.

Shark Measurements

Shark	Average length	Average weight
dwarf dogfish	6 inches (15 cm)	1.5 ounces (43 g)
cookie-cutter shark	20 inches (50 cm)	5.5 ounces (156 g)
bullhead shark	40 inches (1 m)	20 pounds (9 kg)
angel shark	5 feet (1.5 m)	66 pounds (30 kg)
thresher shark	15 feet (4.5 m)	350 pounds (159 kg)
Greenland shark	20 feet (6 m)	2,200 pounds (998 kg)
great white shark	20 feet (6 m)	7,000 pounds (3,200 kg)
basking shark	33 feet (10 m)	15,400 pounds (6,985 kg)
whale shark	40 feet (12 m)	28,700 pounds (13,018 kg)

Think About It!

How are all the sharks in this passage similar?

All About Sharks

Ancient Sharks

Different species of sharks have existed in the ocean for almost 400 million years. The megalodon shark lived 1.6 to 16 million years ago. The megalodon measured up to 50 feet (15 meters) in length, its jaws were 6.5 feet (2 meters) wide, and its teeth were up to 8 inches (20 centimeters) long. It weighed around 20 tons (18,144 kilograms), which is as much as five elephants! A megalodon shark was approximately three times the length of a great white shark.

Dorsal Fins

Shark	Height of Dorsal Fin
dwarf dogfish	2.5 cm
cookie-cutter shark	3.75 cm
angel shark	10 cm
bullhead shark	20 cm
thresher shark	33 cm
Greenland shark	50 cm
basking shark	100 cm
great white shark	100 cm
whale shark	228 cm

Shark Parts

Today, more than half of all shark species are smaller than 3 feet (1 meter) long, but some species grow much larger and have unusual features. The hammerhead shark has eyes on the ends of its head and swings its head from side to side to see. Its head can grow up to half as long as its body. Thresher sharks use their tails to slap and lacerate other fish, which causes their prey to be more easily caught and devoured. Their tails can grow as long as their bodies.

Sharks regularly lose their teeth when catching their prey, so they are continually growing replacement teeth. Sharks can have up to 3,000 teeth at a time. Shark teeth often grow in rows of five, and a shark can go through 30,000 teeth in a lifetime!

The fin on top of a shark's back is called the *dorsal fin*. It is this fin that can frequently be seen above the water. Dorsal fins are rigid and support the shark in staying upright in the water. All sharks have one or two dorsal fins.

Types of Sharks

The whale shark is the biggest fish in the world, growing more than 40 feet (12 meters) long and weighing up to 13 tons (about 11,793 kilogram). However, whale sharks are slow swimmers, with a top speed of merely 3 miles per hour (5 kilometers per hour). Whale sharks swim with their mouths open to suck in water that is filled with plankton and small fish. Whale sharks' mouths can be 5 feet (1.5 meters) wide and can suck in over 1,500 gallons (5,678 liters) of water an hour.

The great white shark is one of the most legendary species of shark. Movies have even been created about them! Most great white sharks grow between 12 and 20 feet (about 3.5 to 6 meters) long, which is about as long as a van. Great white sharks are remarkable hunters. They can reach speeds of 25 miles per hour (40 kilometers per hour) and can leap out of the water to catch their prey.

The swell shark sucks water in when it is frightened. It can blow itself up to three times its usual size. It can wedge itself between rocks so no predator can reach it.

A cookie-cutter shark has long, sharp teeth and is able to bite and hold on to bigger prey. When it releases the prey, the bite resembles a cookie shape.

Shark Measurements

Shark	Average length	Average weight
dwarf dogfish	6 inches (15 cm)	1.5 ounces (43 g)
cookie-cutter shark	20 inches (50 cm)	5.5 ounces (156 g)
bullhead shark	40 inches (1 m)	20 pounds (9 kg)
angel shark	5 feet (1.5 m)	66 pounds (30 kg)
thresher shark	15 feet (4.5 m)	350 pounds (159 kg)
Greenland shark	20 feet (6 m)	2,200 pounds (998 kg)
great white shark	20 feet (6 m)	7,000 pounds (3,200 kg)
basking shark	33 feet (10 m)	15,400 pounds (6,985 kg)
whale shark	40 feet (12 m)	28,700 pounds (13,018 kg)

Think About It!

How does a shark's size, teeth, and fin help it survive in the ocean?

The Bread Book

A Slice of Bread

Bread is one of the world's most important foods. It is also one of the most useful. Most people eat bread every day. Today, people can buy bread from stores or bakeries. Some people even bake bread at home.

The U.S. government helps people make healthy food choices. It says that people should eat 3 ounces (85 grams) of whole-grain food each day. One slice of whole-wheat bread weighs 1 ounce (28 grams). So you could eat three slices of whole-wheat bread. This would meet the amount needed each day.

Bread is made in many shapes and sizes. Take a look at a loaf of bread. What shape does it remind you of? It is probably shaped like a rectangular prism. This shape is great for making sandwiches.

What Is in Bread?

Flour is a main part of bread. If you add water, yeast, and some salt to the flour, you have made a loaf of bread! Wheat flour is made from ground wheat. Long ago, people used stones to grind the wheat into flour. Today, the wheat is sent to mills. At mills, it is turned into flour.

Wheat is a grain. The head of the wheat has seeds called *kernels*. The kernels are sent to flour mills. Milling turns the kernels into flour. Wheat can be measured in bushels.

One bushel of wheat:

- contains approximately 1 million kernels
- weighs approximately 60 pounds (27 kilograms)
- produces 42 loaves of white bread
- produces 90 loaves of whole-wheat bread

The Wheat Farmer

Farmers grow wheat. The wheat is harvested. Then it is sent to a flour mill. The wheat grains are broken down. Then they are turned into flour. Bakeries buy the flour to make loaves of bread. Many of the loaves are sold to grocery stores. Let's say a 1-pound (0.5-kilogram) loaf costs around $1.00. The wheat farmer gets about 5 cents of that $1.00. Look at the graph on the previous page to see where the rest of the money goes.

A Baker's Dozen

People often order loaves of bread by the dozen. Normally, 12 items make a dozen. Around the thirteenth century, this changed. Bakers began to add an extra loaf to every dozen. They did not want to be accused of cheating people. So "13 items" has become known as a *baker's dozen*.

Think About It!

What are the steps involved in making bread?

The Bread Book

A Slice of Bread

Bread is one of the world's most important and useful foods. Most people eat some type of bread every day. Today, people can purchase bread from stores or from independent bakeries. Some people even bake bread at home.

The U.S. government helps people make healthy food choices. It suggests people eat 3 ounces (85 grams) of whole-grain food each day. One slice of whole-wheat bread weighs 1 ounce (28 grams). So if you ate three slices of whole-wheat bread, this would meet the needed daily requirement.

Bread is made in many shapes and sizes. Take a look at a loaf of bread—what shape does it remind you of? It is probably shaped like a rectangular prism because this shape is perfect for making sandwiches.

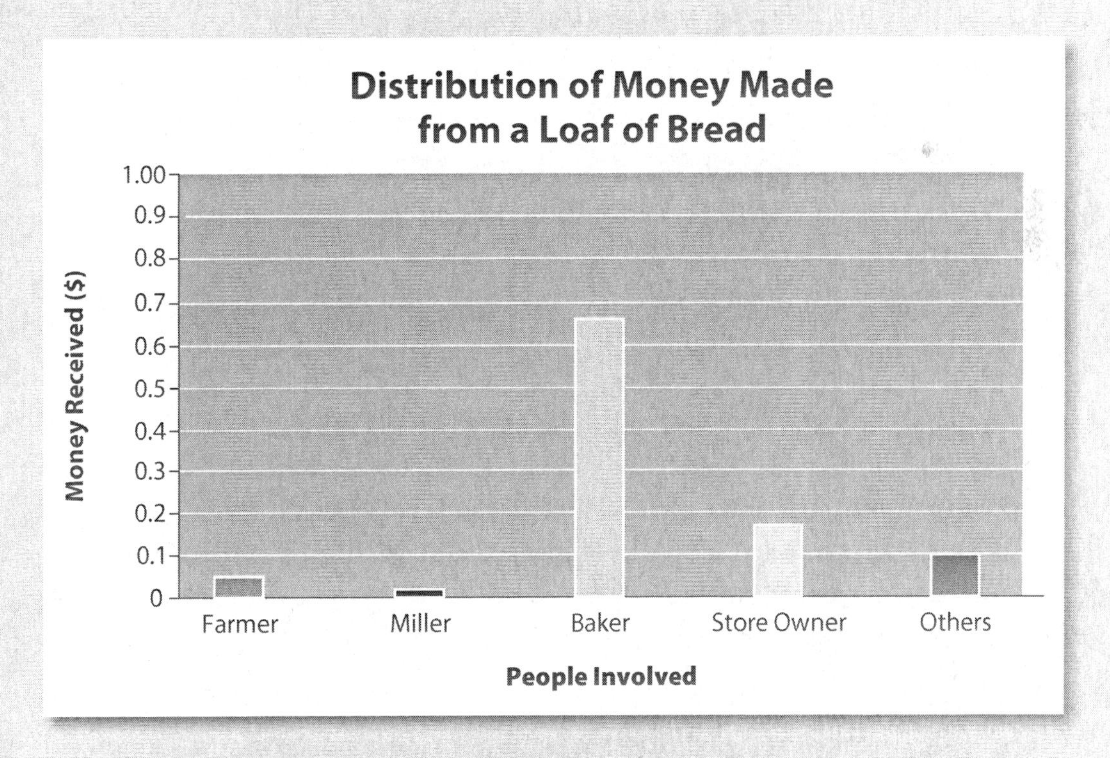

What Is in Bread?

Flour is a main ingredient of bread. Add water, yeast, and some salt to the flour, and you have made a simple loaf of bread! Wheat flour is made from ground wheat. Long ago, people used stones to grind the wheat into flour, but today, the wheat is sent to mills and turned into flour.

Wheat is a grain, and the head of the wheat has seeds called *kernels*. The kernels are sent to flour mills where the milling turns the kernels into flour. Wheat can be measured in bushels.

One bushel of wheat:

- contains approximately 1 million kernels
- weighs approximately 60 pounds (27 kilograms)
- produces 42 loaves of white bread
- produces 90 loaves of whole-wheat bread

The Wheat Farmer

Farmers grow wheat. The wheat is harvested, and then it is sent to a flour mill. The wheat grains are broken down and turned into flour. Bakeries buy the flour to make loaves of bread. Many of the loaves of bread are then sold to grocery stores. Let's say a 1-pound (0.5-kilograms) loaf costs around $1.00; the wheat farmer gets about 5 cents of that $1.00. Look at the graph on the previous page to show you where the remainder of the money goes.

A Baker's Dozen

People often order loaves of bread by the dozen. Normally, 12 items make a dozen. Around the thirteenth century, bakers began to add an extra loaf to every dozen. They did not want to be accused of cheating the customers. So "13 items" has become known as a *baker's dozen*.

Think About It!

Why do you think one bushel of wheat produces more whole-wheat bread than white bread?

The Bread Book

A Slice of Bread

Bread has historically been one of the world's most important and convenient foods. Most of the population eats some variety of bread every day. Today, people can purchase bread from stores or from independent bakeries. Some people even choose to bake bread at home.

The U.S. government assists people in making healthy food selections. It suggests everyone eat 3 ounces (85 grams) of whole-grain food each day. One slice of whole-wheat bread weighs 1 ounce (28 grams). So if you consumed three slices of whole-wheat bread, this would fulfill the required daily recommendation.

Bread is made in various shapes and sizes. Observe the appearance of a loaf of bread—what shape does it resemble? It is probably shaped like a rectangular prism because this shape is suitable for making sandwiches.

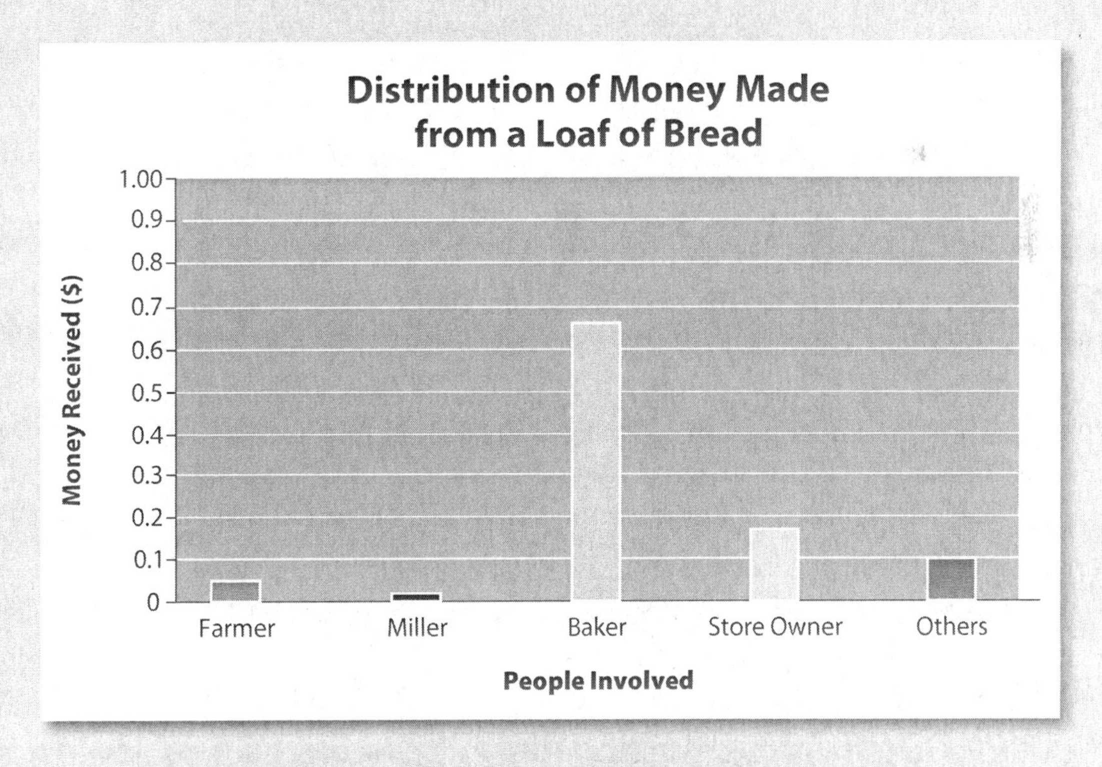

What Is in Bread?

Flour is the major ingredient of bread; add water, yeast, and some salt to the flour, and you have made an ordinary loaf of bread! Wheat flour is created from ground-up wheat. Long ago, people used stones to grind the wheat into flour, but today, the wheat is dispatched to mills and turned into flour.

Wheat is a grain, and the head of the wheat has seeds called *kernels*. The kernels are sent to flour mills where the milling turns the kernels into flour. Wheat can be measured in bushels.

One bushel of wheat:

- contains approximately 1 million kernels
- weighs approximately 60 pounds (27 kilograms)
- produces 42 loaves of white bread
- produces 90 loaves of whole-wheat bread.

The Wheat Farmer

Farmers cultivate wheat. The wheat is harvested and then sent to a flour mill where the wheat grains are broken down and turned into flour. Bakeries purchase the flour and bake loaves of bread. Numerous loaves of bread are then sold to grocery stores. Let's estimate a 1-pound (0.5-kilogram) loaf of bread has a purchase price of around $1.00; the wheat farmer receives only about 5 cents of that $1.00. Look at the graph on the previous page to determine where the remainder of the money goes.

A Baker's Dozen

People frequently order loaves of bread by the dozen, and normally, 12 items make that dozen. Around the thirteenth century, though, bakers began to add an additional loaf to every dozen because they did not want to be accused of cheating the customers. So "13 items" has become accepted as a *baker's dozen*.

Think About It!

If you could invent a new shape for loaves of bread, what would it be? Why?

Producers and Consumers

Producers

There is no start in a cycle. But we need to begin somewhere. So let's start with producers. In the nutrient cycle, producers take nonliving things. They use them to make what they need. They do this so they can grow and live. They make nutrients for themselves. In other words, they make their own food. To do that, they need the sun's energy.

The sun gives off energy every day. Earth gets some of it. This makes life on Earth possible. The energy warms the ground. It also warms oceans and lakes. Plants get this energy. They use it to help them live and grow. They grow stems, trunks, branches, and leaves. They make their own fuel that powers all this growing. They make their fuel using energy from the sun. Produce is another word for make. Plants make their own fuel. Because of this, they are called *producers*.

Getting Energy

Animals are not like plants. They can't use energy straight from the sun. They can't make the things their bodies need. The sun's energy can't fuel what their bodies need to do. Their bodies need to breathe, move, and release waste.

Plants are producers.

We know plants store energy. They also have nutrients. Many animals must eat plants to stay alive. They use plant parts for growing. They also use them to take care of their own bodies. Eating plants for their nutrients has a name. It is called *consumption*. All animals are consumers. They consume their nutrients. This includes humans. Animals need nutrients to grow and to keep their bodies healthy. Nutrients exist in many forms. Animals have different ways of getting them. But there are two main ways they do this. Both involve eating.

Types of Consumers

Some animals eat parts of plants. This is how they get their nutrients. They may eat roots, stems, or leaves. They eat fruits, flowers, nectar, and seeds, too. Every creature has its favorites. Some eat the whole plant! These animals are called *herbivores*.

The other way for animals to get nutrients is by eating other animals. They are meat eaters. They mostly hunt and kill their prey. But some eat meat that has been killed by other animals. They also eat meat that dies naturally. These creatures are scavengers. These animals are called *carnivores*.

Many animals use plants and animals to get nutrients. They eat both. These animals are called *omnivores*. Humans are animals. Which type are we? We eat plants such as carrots, peas, onions, and corn. We can also eat many kinds of meats such as chicken, fish, pork, and beef. We eat plants and animals. So we are omnivores. Other omnivores include bears, pigs, dogs, foxes, and badgers.

Animals are consumers.

Think About It!

Define the three types of consumers: herbivore, carnivore, and omnivore.

Producers and Consumers

Producers

There's no beginning in a cycle. But we need to start somewhere. So let's begin with producers. In the nutrient cycle, producers take basic, nonliving substances. They use them to make what they need to grow and live. They make nutrients for themselves. In other words, they make their own food. To do that, they need the sun's energy.

Energy radiates outward from the sun every day. Earth receives some of this energy. It makes life on Earth possible. The energy warms the ground. It also warms oceans and lakes. Plants get this energy and use it to help them live. They use this energy to grow. They use it to make their stems and trunks, branches and leaves, and flowers and fruit. They also make their own fuel that powers all this growing. Since plants produce, or make, their own fuel, they are called *producers*. They make their fuel using energy from the sun.

Getting Energy

Animals can't use energy straight from the sun like plants can. They can't make the basic materials their bodies need. They don't use the sun's energy to power what their bodies need to do—breathe, move, and release waste.

As we know, plants store energy in their parts. They also have nutrients. Many animals must eat plants to stay alive. They use plant materials for growing and taking care of their own bodies. This process of eating plants for their nutrients is called *consumption*. The animals are consumers. They consume their nutrients. All animals are consumers, including humans. Animals need nutrients to grow and keep their body tissues healthy.

Nutrients exist in many forms. Animals have developed different ways of getting those nutrients. But there are two main ways that animals do this. Both involve eating.

Types of Consumers

One way animals get their nutrients is by eating different parts of plants. These animals are called *herbivores*. Herbivores may eat roots, stems, leaves, fruits, flowers, nectar, or seeds. Every animal has its preferences. Some eat the entire plant!

The other way for animals to get nutrients is by eating other animals. These animals are called *carnivores*. They are meat eaters. These animals mainly hunt and kill their prey. But some carnivores eat prey that has been killed by other animals or that dies naturally. These animals are scavengers.

Many animals actually use both ways to get their nutrients. They eat plants and they eat other animals. These animals are called *omnivores*. Humans are animals. Which type of consumer are we? We eat plants such as carrots, peas, broccoli, and corn. We can also eat many kinds of meats such as chicken, fish, pork, and beef. Since we eat plants and animals, we are omnivores. Other omnivores include bears, pigs, dogs, foxes, and badgers.

Think About It!

Why must animals eat plants or other animals?

Animals are consumers.

Producers and Consumers

Producers

There's no beginning in a cycle, but we need to start somewhere. So let's begin with producers. In the nutrient cycle, producers take basic nonliving substances and use them to create what they need to grow and live. They make nutrients for themselves—in other words, they make their own food. To do that, they require the sun's energy.

Energy radiates outward from the sun every day. Earth receives some of this energy, which makes life on Earth possible. The energy warms the ground and also warms oceans and lakes. Plants acquire this energy and use it to help them live. They use this energy to grow and to make their stems and trunks, branches and leaves, and flowers and fruit. They also make their own fuel that powers all this growing. Since plants produce, or make, their own fuel, they are called *producers*. They make their fuel using energy from the sun.

Getting Energy

Animals are unable to use energy straight from the sun like plants can. They can't make the elementary materials their bodies need. They can't use the sun's energy to power what their bodies need to do—breathe, move, and release waste.

As we know, plants store energy in their parts, but they also have nutrients. Many animals must eat plants to stay alive, and they use plant materials for growing and taking care of their own bodies. This process of eating plants for their nutrients is called *consumption*. The animals are consumers, so they consume their nutrients. All animals are consumers, including humans. Animals need nutrients to grow and keep their body tissues healthy. Nutrients are available in many forms, and animals have developed different methods for receiving those nutrients. But there are two leading ways that animals do this, and both involve eating.

Types of Consumers

One way animals get their nutrients is by eating different portions of plants. These animals are called *herbivores*. Herbivores may eat roots, stems, leaves, fruits, flowers, nectar, or seeds. Every animal has its preferences. Some eat the entire plant!

The other way for animals to get nutrients is by eating other animals. These animals are meat eaters and are called *carnivores*. They primarily hunt and kill their prey, but some carnivores eat prey that has been killed by other animals or that dies naturally. These animals are scavengers.

Many animals actually use both ways to obtain their nutrients. They eat plants and other animals, so these animals are called *omnivores*. Humans are animals, but which type of consumer are we? We can eat plants such as carrots, peas, broccoli, and corn. However, we can also eat many kinds of meats such as chicken, fish, pork, and beef. Since we eat plants and animals, we are omnivores. Other omnivores include bears, pigs, dogs, foxes, and badgers.

Animals are consumers.

Think About It!

What might happen to the cycle of life if all plants disappeared?

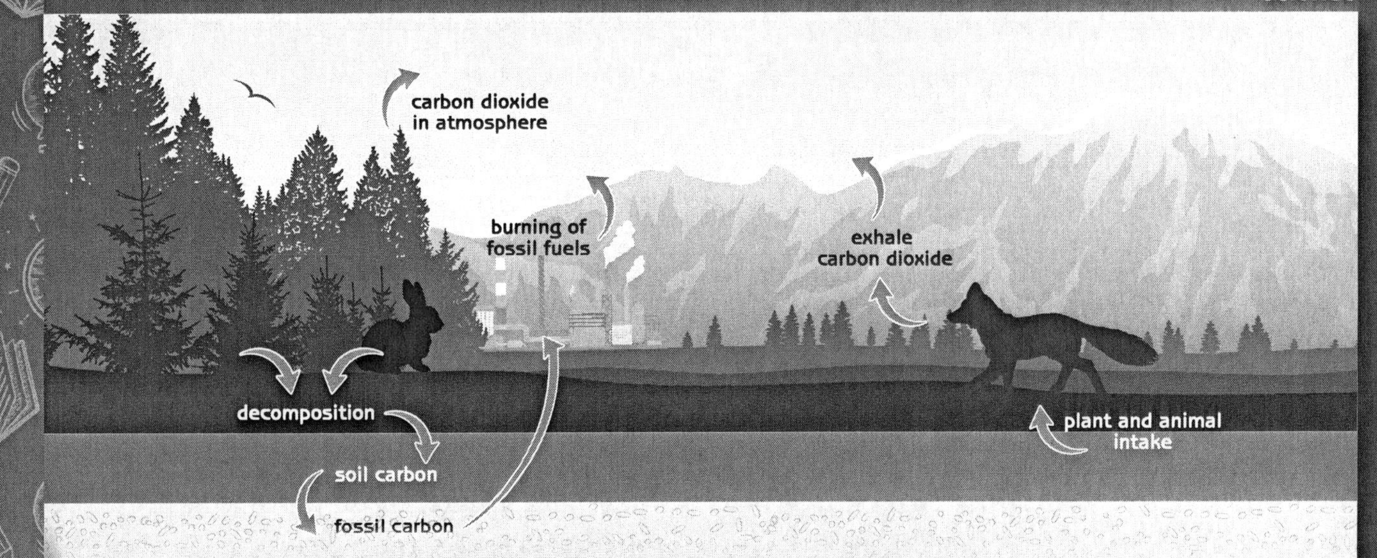

The Nutrient Cycle

Nitrogen Cycle

Nitrogen is all around us. But you'd never know it! This gas has no color, taste, or odor. It is in the air we breathe. About 78 percent of it is this gas. It is a vital element to Earth. All living things use it. Plants can't grow without it.

There is a lot of nitrogen in the air. Most living things need it in a special form. Bacteria have an important job. It makes nitrogen something that living things can use. This process starts in the soil. The nitrogen becomes ammonia. (Yes, it is just like the smelly cleaner in your house!) But ammonia kills plants. It doesn't help them grow. So a new type of bacteria steps in. It turns the ammonia into nitrates. And plants can use nitrates! The plants use them to create protein. This helps plants grow big and strong. Many animals eat plants. They get the protein from the plants. Then other animals eat them and get the proteins too!

Nitrogen is also part of the inside of plant cells. It is called *chlorophyll*. This is what makes leaves green. It collects energy from the sun. Then it uses the energy. It combines water and carbon dioxide. This makes sugar and oxygen. If there is not enough nitrogen, plants suffer. They may stop growing. Their leaves may turn yellow.

But there's more to the nitrogen cycle. When animals die bacteria, fungi, and worms go to work. These are decomposers. They help break down dead things. This lets the nutrients go back into the earth.

Carbon Cycle

Carbon is found in every living thing on Earth. It is part of the air we breathe. It's in the water we drink. Carbon is in diamonds and the gas in your car. It's even in your pencil! Carbon is an element. It is one of the key elements on Earth.

How do living things get carbon? It starts with photosynthesis. First, a plant uses its roots. It absorbs water and nutrients from soil. Then plants absorb a gas through their leaves. The gas is carbon dioxide (CO_2). Plants use CO_2 and sunlight to make glucose. Glucose is sugar. It gives plants fuel to grow.

Animals eat plants. The carbon passes to them. Animals use carbon. It builds and repairs cells in their bodies. Animals eat other animals. The carbon is passed along.

The carbon cycle is complex. It is more than carbon moving as plants and animals are eaten. When you breathe, you return carbon dioxide to the air. But there's another way carbon gets back to Earth. Plants and animals die. They are buried in the ground. They release carbon. Decomposers break them down. Carbon returns to the soil. Then, more living things can use the carbon. A carbon atom can be used again and again. It recycles itself. It can be part of many plants and animals. This happens over millions of years!

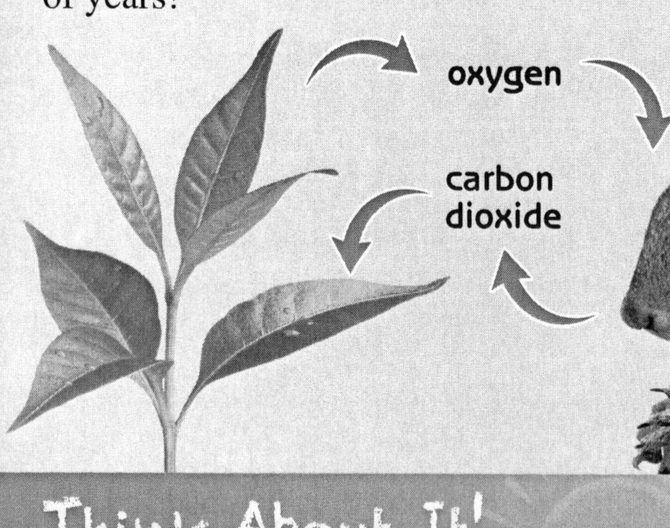

Think About It!

What is nitrogen? What is carbon?

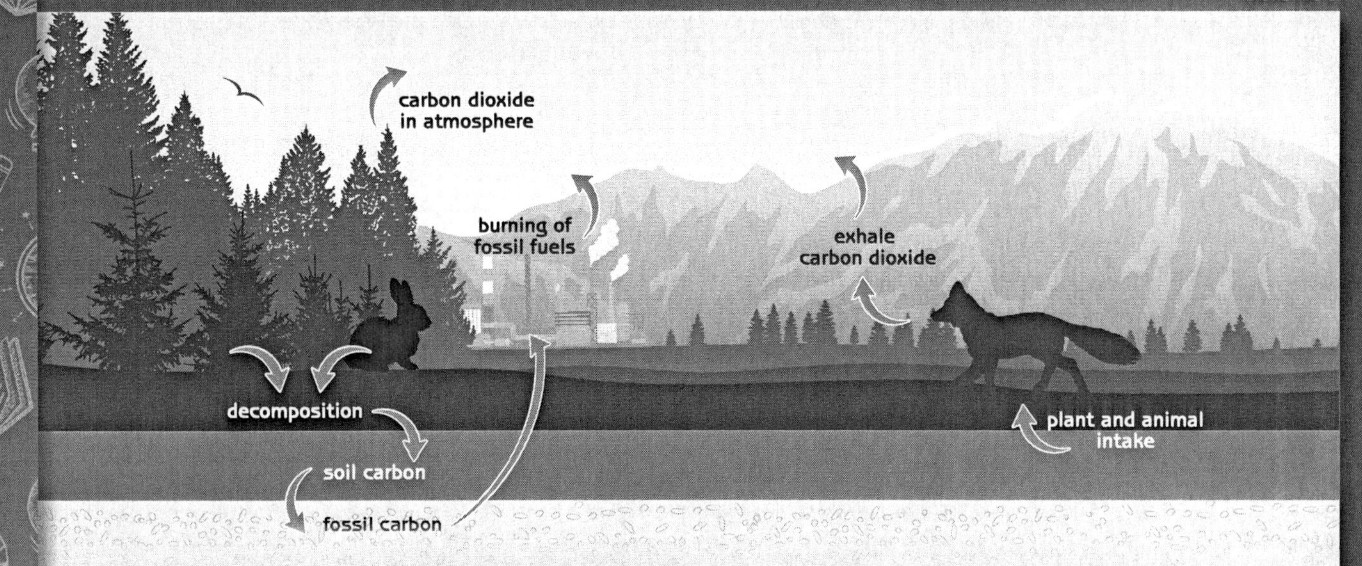

The Nutrient Cycle

Nitrogen Cycle

Nitrogen is all around us. But you'd never know it! This gas has no color, taste, or odor. But 78 percent of the air we breathe is made of it. This gas is one of the most important elements on Earth. All living things use it. Plants can't grow without it.

There is a lot of nitrogen in the air. But most life forms can only use it in a special form. Some bacteria focus on making nitrogen that living things can use. The process starts in the soil. Here, the special bacteria turn the nitrogen into ammonia. (Yes, just like the smelly household cleaner!) But ammonia is better known for killing plants than helping them grow. So another type of bacteria steps in. It turns the ammonia into nitrates. And plants can use nitrates! They use nitrates to create protein. And protein helps them grow big and strong. Many animals eat plants and get the protein as well. Proteins are then moved to larger animals that eat the protein-rich smaller animals.

Nitrogen is also a part of *chlorophyll*. Chlorophyll is found inside plant cells. It is what makes leaves green. It collects energy from the sun. Then it uses it to combine water and carbon dioxide to make sugar and oxygen. If there isn't enough nitrogen in chlorophyll, plants suffer. They may stop growing, and their leaves may turn yellow.

But there's more to the nitrogen cycle. When an animal dies, bacteria, worms, and fungi go to work. These decomposers help break down dead animals. This allows the nutrients in their bodies to go back into the earth.

Carbon Cycle

Carbon is found in every living thing on Earth. It is part of the air we breathe. It's in the water we drink and in shiny diamonds. It's in the gas in your car. Carbon is even in the pencil you write with! Carbon is one of the most important elements on Earth.

But how do living things get carbon? It starts with photosynthesis. First, a plant's roots absorb water and nutrients from soil. Then, plants absorb carbon dioxide (CO_2) through their leaves. Plants use CO_2 and sunlight to make glucose, or sugar. Glucose gives plants fuel to grow.

Carbon gets passed to animals when they eat plants. Animals use carbon to build and repair cells in their bodies. When animals eat other animals, the carbon keeps getting passed along.

The carbon cycle doesn't just involve the movement of carbon as plants and animals are eaten. When you exhale, you return carbon dioxide into the air. But there's also another way that carbon is returned to Earth. When plants and the animals that eat them die, they are buried in the ground. They also release carbon. Decomposers break them down and return carbon to the soil. Then, the carbon can be used by more living things. A carbon atom can be used again and again. It recycles itself. It can be part of many different plants and animals over millions of years!

Think About It!

Why are nitrogen and carbon two of the most important elements on Earth?

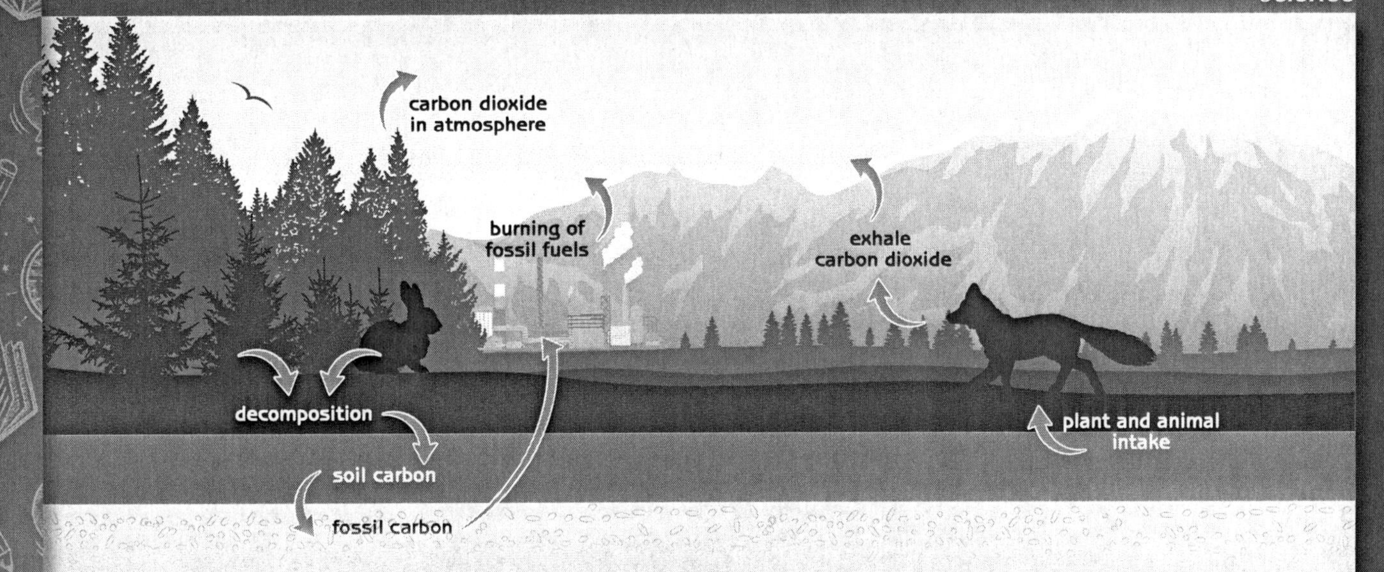

The Nutrient Cycle

Nitrogen Cycle

Nitrogen is all around us, but you'd never know it! This gas is colorless, tasteless, and odorless. But 78 percent of the atmosphere is made of it. Nitrogen is one of the most important elements on Earth because all living things use it. In fact, plants can't grow without it.

There may be a lot of nitrogen in the air, but the majority of life forms can only use nitrogen in a particular form. There are bacteria that specialize in producing nitrogen that living things can use. The process starts in the soil. Here, the special bacteria turn the nitrogen into ammonia. (Yes, just like the smelly household cleaner!) But ammonia is better known for killing plants than helping them grow, so another type of bacteria steps in. It turns the ammonia into nitrates—and plants can use nitrates! They use nitrates to create protein, and protein helps them grow big and strong. Many animals eat plants and get the protein as well. Proteins are then moved to larger animals that eat the protein-rich smaller animals.

Nitrogen is also a part of *chlorophyll*, which is found inside plant cells. It is what causes leaves to be green. It collects energy from the sun and uses it to combine water and carbon dioxide to make sugar and oxygen. If there isn't enough nitrogen in chlorophyll, plants suffer. They may stop growing, and their leaves may turn yellow.

But there's more to the nitrogen cycle. When an animal dies, bacteria, worms, and fungi go to work. These decomposers help break down dead animals and allow the nutrients in their bodies to go back into the earth.

Carbon Cycle

Carbon is found in every living thing on Earth. It is part of the air we breathe, it's in the water we drink, it's in shiny diamonds, and it's in the gas that powers cars. It's even in the pencil you write with! Carbon is one of the most important elements on Earth.

But how do living things get carbon? It starts with photosynthesis. First, a plant's roots absorb water and nutrients from soil. Then, plants absorb carbon dioxide (CO_2) through their leaves. Plants use CO_2 and sunlight to make glucose, or sugar, which gives plants fuel to grow.

Carbon gets passed to animals when they eat plants. Animals use carbon to build and repair cells in their bodies. When animals eat other animals, the carbon keeps getting passed along.

The carbon cycle doesn't just involve the movement of carbon as plants and animals are eaten. When you exhale, you return carbon dioxide into the air. But there's also another way that carbon is returned to Earth. When plants and the animals that eat them die and are buried in the ground, they also release carbon. Decomposers break them down and return carbon to the soil. Then, the carbon can be used by more living things. A carbon atom can be used again and again. It recycles itself and can be part of many different organisms over millions of years!

Think About It!

What are the most important parts of the carbon and nitrogen cycles?

Circuits

Series Circuits

A series circuit only has one electrical pathway. That's why they are easy to make! All you need in the circuit can be lined up on the same wire. But if one part fails, they all do.

The diagram shows a string of lights. They are in a series circuit. All the light bulbs are in a long line. It's too bad they don't always work well. Light bulbs are like batteries. They don't last forever. Bulbs have filaments. This is a small piece of metal that lights the bulb. It can burn out. Then the circuit breaks.

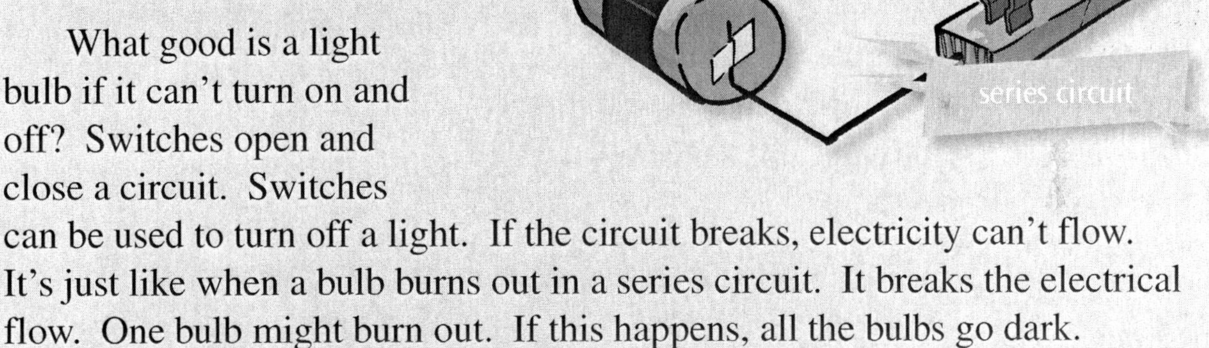

Switches

What good is a light bulb if it can't turn on and off? Switches open and close a circuit. Switches can be used to turn off a light. If the circuit breaks, electricity can't flow. It's just like when a bulb burns out in a series circuit. It breaks the electrical flow. One bulb might burn out. If this happens, all the bulbs go dark.

Parallel Circuits

Parallel circuits have more than one electrical pathway to move along. There might be more than one path. If so, it's a parallel circuit. That's how it gets its name. Most houses are wired with parallel circuits. This is because one bulb might go out. But it doesn't take the whole circuit with it. You wouldn't want all the lights to go out when you turn off the TV. Parallel circuits keep the lights on.

There are many paths electricity can take in this type of circuit. Electric current travels the loop. It must enter by a single resistor. By the laws of physics, it has to travel through the path of least resistance. The current for both paths can be the same. Then it will split evenly through each resistor. One resistor might be disconnected. Then it will choose the other path. This is what allows the circuit to continue.

Complex Circuits

We've looked at series circuits. We've looked at parallel circuits. But circuits aren't always that simple. They can have both series and parallel parts. These are *complex circuits*. It's useful to study both kinds. They help us learn how electricity works. Most electronics have complex circuits. Laptops have them. Phones have them, too!

Short Circuits

Watch out for a short circuit! It's when part of a circuit is not joined the right way. The drawing shows a poorly made circuit. Here, one of the basic parts is missing. A circuit should have three things. One is a power source. The next is a connection. And the third is the thing getting the power. But here, the power source and the thing getting the power are the same. It's a battery! The electricity does not travel through a light bulb. Instead, the circuit tells it to take a shortcut. It travels from one end of the battery to the next. The battery gets a large jolt of electricity. It overheats and a fire may start.

Think About It!

What are circuits?

Circuits

Series Circuits

A series circuit has only one electrical pathway. That's why they're easy to make! Everything you need in the circuit can be lined up on the same wire. But that means that if one component fails, they all do.

The diagram shows a string of lights that are in a series circuit. All the light bulbs are lined up in a long series. Unfortunately, they don't always work well. Light bulbs are like batteries. They don't last forever. Over time, the filament will burn out. The filament is a small piece of metal that lights the bulb. This breaks the circuit.

series circuit

Switches

What good is a light bulb if it can't be turned on and off? Switches open and close a circuit. Switches can be used to turn a light bulb off. When the circuit is broken, the electricity can't flow. It's just like when a bulb burns out in a series circuit. It breaks the electrical flow. If one bulb burns out, all the bulbs go dark.

Parallel Circuits

Parallel circuits have more than one electrical pathway to move along. If there is more than one path, then it's a parallel circuit—hence the name. Most households are wired with parallel circuits. That way, if one bulb goes out, it doesn't take the whole circuit with it. You wouldn't want all the lights in your house to go out when you turn off the TV. Parallel circuits keep the lights on.

There are multiple paths electricity can take in a parallel circuit. As electric current travels the loop, it must enter through a single resistor. By the laws of physics, it has to travel through the path of least resistance. If the current for both paths is the same, then it will split evenly through each resistor. If one resistor is disconnected, then it will choose the other path. This is what allows the circuit to continue.

Complex Circuits

We've looked at series circuits. We've looked at parallel circuits. But circuits aren't always that simple. Sometimes, they have both series and parallel parts. These are *complex circuits*. It's useful to study simple series circuits and parallel circuits. They help us understand how electricity works. But most electronics have complex circuits. Computers have complex circuits. So do phones!

Short Circuits

A short circuit occurs when a part of a circuit is not connected properly. The drawing shows a poorly made circuit. Here, one of the basic parts is missing. A circuit should include three things. They are a power source, a connection, and the thing getting the power. But here, the power source and the thing getting the power are the same thing. It's a battery! The electricity does not travel through a light bulb. Instead, the circuit directs it to take a shortcut. It travels from one end of the battery to the next. The battery gets a large jolt of electricity. It overheats and a fire may start.

Think About It!

Compare and contrast series and parallel circuits.

Circuits

Series Circuits

A series circuit has only one electrical pathway. That's why they're simple to make! Everything you need in the circuit can be lined up on the same wire; but that means if one component fails, they all do.

The diagram shows a string of lights in a series circuit. All the light bulbs are lined up in a long series. Unfortunately, they don't always work well. Like batteries, light bulbs don't last forever. Over time, the filament, which is a small piece of metal that lights the bulb, will burn out, and this breaks the circuit.

series circuit

Switches

What good is a light bulb if it can't be turned on and off? Switches open and close a circuit. Switches can be used to turn a light bulb off. When the circuit is broken, the electricity can't flow. It's just like when a bulb burns out in a series circuit—it breaks the electrical flow. If one bulb burns out, all the bulbs go dark.

Parallel Circuits

Parallel circuits have more than one electrical pathway to move along. If there is more than one path, then it's a parallel circuit—hence the name. Most households are wired with parallel circuits because if one bulb goes out, it doesn't take the whole circuit with it. You wouldn't want all the lights in your house to go out when you turn off the TV. Parallel circuits keep the lights on.

There are multiple paths electricity can take in a parallel circuit. As electric current travels the loop, it must enter through a single resistor. By the laws of physics, it has to travel through the path of least resistance. If the current for both paths is the same, then it will split evenly through each resistor. If one resistor is disconnected, then it will choose the other path. This is what allows the circuit to continue.

Complex Circuits

We've looked at series circuits, and we've looked at parallel circuits. But circuits aren't always that simple. Sometimes, they have both series and parallel parts, which are called *complex circuits*. It's useful to study simple series circuits and parallel circuits because they help us understand how electricity works. But most electronics have complex circuits. Computers have complex circuits, and so do phones!

Short Circuits

A short circuit occurs when a part of a circuit is not connected properly. The illustration shows a poorly made circuit with one of the basic parts missing. A circuit should include a power source, a connection, and the object receiving the power. But here, the power source and the object receiving the power are the same object: a battery. Instead of sending the electricity through a light bulb, the circuit directs it to take a shortcut, and it travels from one end of the battery to the next. The battery gets a large jolt of electricity, it overheats, and a fire may start.

Think About It!

What are some examples of circuits that you use in your daily life?

Sound Waves and Communication

Measuring Sound

We don't often see or feel sound. We hear it. The human ear responds to changes in pressure waves. It senses that as sound. Clap your hands. Is the sound loud? Could you clap more loudly?

Volume is how loud a sound is. It results from how close the molecules are. The more energy a vibration has, the closer the particles. More energy also means a louder sound. You might turn up the volume on your TV. You increase the power of the vibration. Your action packs the molecules very close. That makes the sound louder.

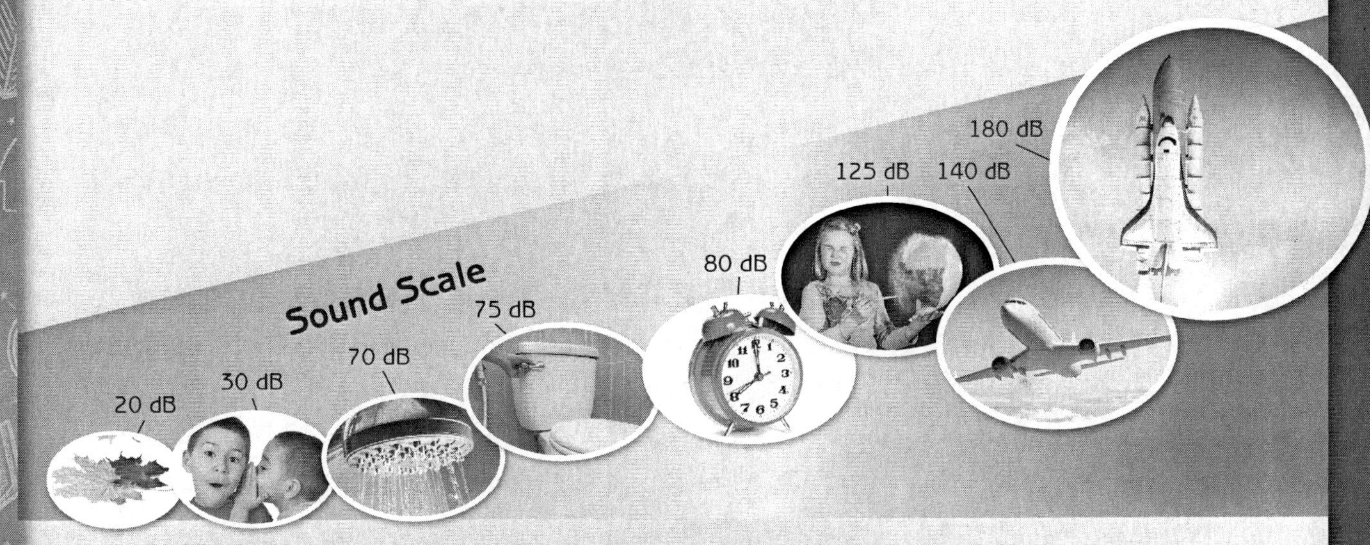

We measure a sound's volume in decibels (dB). This is a measure of strength. It tells us how much energy a sound wave has. The quietest sounds we can hear are about 10 dB. This is the sound of normal breathing. A whisper has a low strength. It measures about 30 dB. Talking has a little more strength. That sound is 40 dB. Talking is only 10 dB louder than a whisper. But each 10 dB of sound multiplies its strength by 10. So talking is 100 times stronger. Sounds of 130 dB can be painful. A jet plane takes off at about 140 dB.

The amount of energy isn't the only thing we measure about sound. We also look at wavelength. That's the distance between the two peaks of the same wave. Waves can be short and close to each other. They can be long and spread apart. Some waves are short. So the sound has a high frequency. Frequency is how many times a particle vibrates in a second. A high frequency has a high pitch. A whistle has a high pitch. So we know it also has a high frequency.

Short wavelengths make high frequencies. Their pitch is shrill. A mouse's squeak is a shrill noise. Long wavelengths make low frequencies. Their pitch is deep. A lion's roar is a deep noise. Frequency is measured in hertz (Hz). Humans can hear sounds between 20 Hz and 20,000 Hz. The intensity of a sound can vary with distance. Decibels decrease when we are far from the sound's source. This is because the wave loses energy. But frequency and pitch remain constant. The wavelength of a sound doesn't change. Even losing energy does not change the length.

Sometimes, it seems like the pitch of a sound rises and falls. This occurs when the sound's source is moving. Watch an auto race on TV. Listen as the cars pass by. The vroom of the engine changes when they pass. It starts at a higher pitch when it's coming closer. Then it's in front of the viewer. The pitch is true to life. As the vehicle leaves, the pitch seems to drop lower.

The same thing happens with ambulances or police cars. When their sirens approach, it sounds very shrill. Then they pass and the pitch seems to grow deeper. This an example of the Doppler effect.

When a sound's source is moving, it sends out a sound wave. Then it travels a short way before the next wave. So the waves in front of the source become pressed together. The waves behind become stretched apart. So the wavelengths in front of the source are shorter. And the pitch is higher. The wavelengths behind the source are longer. And the pitch is lower.

Think About It!

How is sound measured?

Sound Waves and Communication

Measuring Sound

We don't often see or feel sound. We hear it. The human ear responds to changes in pressure waves. And it senses that as sound. When you clap your hands, is the sound loud? Could you clap more loudly?

The loudness, or volume, of a sound results from how tightly the molecules are pressed together. The more energy a vibration has, the tighter the particles and the louder the sound. When you turn up the volume on your TV, you increase the energy of the vibration. Your action packs the molecules more tightly. That makes the sound louder.

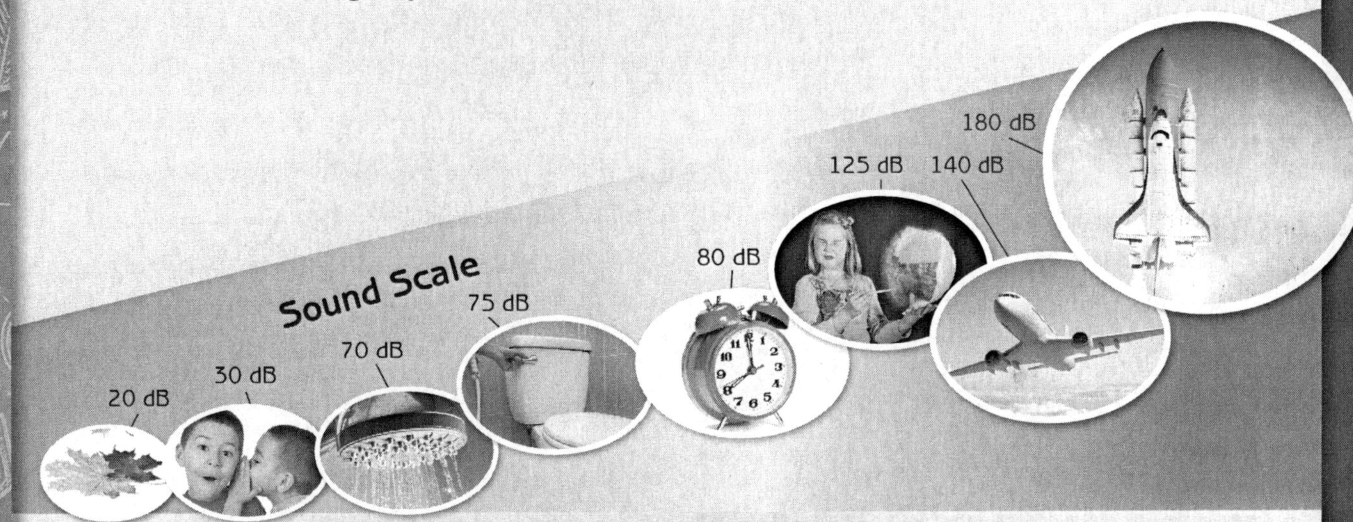

We measure a sound's volume in decibels (dB). This is a measure of intensity that tells us how much energy a sound wave has. The quietest sounds we can hear are about 10 dB. The sound of normal breathing is about 10 dB. A whisper has a low intensity, measuring about 30 dB. When people talk, that sound is 40 dB. Talking is only 10 dB louder than whispering. Each 10 dB of sound multiplies intensity by 10, so talking is 100 times more intense. Sounds of 130 dB can be painful; a jet plane takes off at about 140 dB.

The amount of energy isn't the only thing we measure when it comes to sound. We also look at wavelength. That's the distance between the two peaks of the same wave. Waves can be short and close together. They also can be long and spread apart. When waves are short, sound has a high frequency. Frequency refers to how many times a particle vibrates in a second. A high frequency comes with a high pitch. A whistle has a high pitch, so we know it also has a high frequency.

Short wavelengths create high frequencies. They sound shrill in pitch, like a mouse's squeak. Long wavelengths produce low frequencies. They sound deep in pitch, like a lion's roar. Frequency is measured in hertz (Hz). Humans can detect sounds between 20 Hz and 20,000 Hz. The intensity of a sound can vary with distance. Decibels decrease when we are farther from the sound's source because the wave loses energy. But frequency and pitch remain constant. The wavelength of a sound doesn't alter even when the wave loses energy.

There are times when it seems like the pitch of a sound rises and falls. This occurs when the sound's source is in motion. Watch an auto race on TV and listen as the cars pass by. The vroom of the engine changes when they pass. It starts at a higher pitch when it's approaching. When it's in front of the viewer, the pitch is true to life. And then, as the vehicle leaves, the pitch seems to drop lower.

Emergency vehicles produce a similar effect. When their sirens approach, the sound seems very shrill. But after they pass, the pitch seems to grow deeper. This an example of the Doppler effect at work.

When a sound's source is moving, it sends out a sound wave and then travels a short way before the next wave. So, the waves in front of the source become pressed together, and the waves behind become stretched apart. This makes the wavelengths in front of the source shorter and the pitch higher. The wavelength behind the source is longer, and the pitch is lower.

Think About It!

Describe what happens when the volume of music is turned up.

Sound Waves and Communication

Measuring Sound

We don't regularly see or feel sound—we hear it. The human ear responds to changes in pressure waves, and it senses that as sound. When you clap your hands, is the sound loud? Could you clap more loudly?

The loudness, or volume, of a sound results from how tightly the molecules are pressed together. The more energy a vibration has, the tighter the particles and the louder the sound. When you turn up the volume on your television, you increase the energy of the vibration. Your action packs the molecules more tightly, which makes the sound louder.

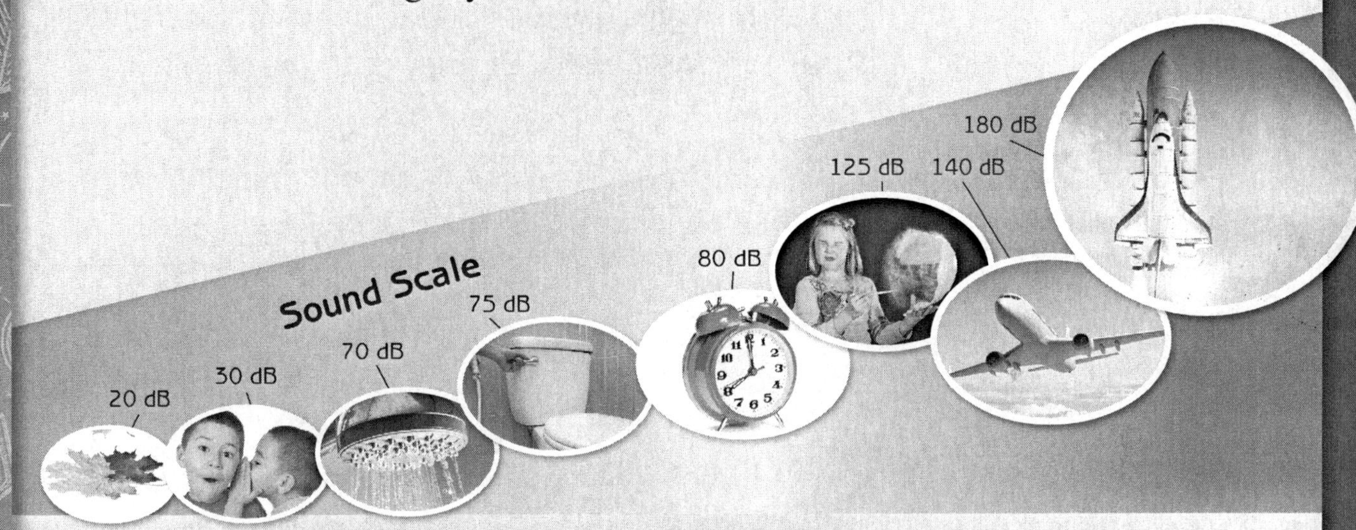

We measure a sound's volume in decibels (dB). This is a measure of intensity that tells us how much energy a sound wave has. The quietest sounds we can hear are approximately 10 dB, the sound of normal breathing. A whisper has a low intensity, measuring about 30 dB. When people talk, that sound is 40 dB. Talking is only 10 dB louder than whispering, but each 10 dB of sound multiplies intensity by 10, so talking is 100 times more intense when compared to whispering. Sounds of 130 dB can be painful; a jet plane takes off at about 140 dB.

The amount of energy isn't the only thing we measure when it comes to sound. We also look at wavelength, which is the distance between the two peaks of the same wave. Waves can be short and close together or long and spread apart. When waves are short, sound has a high frequency. Frequency refers to how many times a particle vibrates in a second. A high frequency comes with a high pitch. A whistle has a high pitch, so we know it also has a high frequency.

Short wavelengths create high frequencies and sound shrill in pitch, like a mouse's squeak. Long wavelengths produce low frequencies and sound deep in pitch, like a lion's roar. Frequency is measured in hertz (Hz). Humans can detect sounds between 20 Hz and 20,000 Hz. The intensity of a sound can vary with distance. Decibels decrease when we are farther from the sound's source because the wave loses energy, but frequency and pitch remain constant. The wavelength of a sound doesn't alter even when the wave's energy diminishes.

There are times when the pitch of a sound gives the impression of rising and falling. This occurs when the sound's source is in motion. Watch an auto race on television and listen as the cars pass by. The vroom of the engine changes when they pass. It begins at a higher pitch when the car is approaching, the pitch is true to life when it's in front of the viewer, and then, as the vehicle leaves, the pitch seems to drop lower.

Emergency vehicles produce a similar effect. When their sirens approach, the sound seems very shrill, but after they pass, the pitch seems to grow deeper. This an example of the Doppler effect at work.

When a sound's source is moving, it sends out a sound wave and travels a short way before the next wave. So the waves in front of the source become pressed together, and the waves behind become stretched apart. This makes the wavelengths in front of the source shorter and the pitch higher. The wavelength behind the source is longer, and the pitch is lower.

Think About It!

Some physicians tell people to limit the time they wear headphones to one hour a day. They request you keep headphones at moderate levels. Why do you think physicians are so concerned about these things?

The Story of Fossil Fuels

What Are Fossil Fuels?

Fossil fuels are things like coal, natural gas, and petroleum. We use them every day. They are called fossil fuels for a reason. They are made from organisms that died many years ago. They were buried under layers of dirt and rock. The layers are called *sediment*. They are fuels because they give energy. It powers most of our needs.

Petroleum is a fossil fuel. It is made from very small creatures. They lived in the oceans long ago. Coal is made from plants and animals that lived on land. Natural gas is made in both places. They are found both in oceans and on land. But these fuels have one thing in common. The live beings that made them lived and died long ago. They died hundreds of millions of years ago!

The world has energy demands. And all these fuels provide for them. They are a resource. But they are nonrenewable. That means they are not easy to renew, or refill. It will take many millions of years to make more.

How Are Fossil Fuels Made?

Petroleum and natural gas are fossil fuels. They are made from plants and animals. They died hundreds of millions of years ago. Back then, very small plants and animals floated in the oceans. They were much like the ones we know now. The plants are phytoplankton. They were able to use photosynthesis just like other plants. The animals are zooplankton. They ate other tiny animals. They also ate living and dead plants. They were tiny. But there were billions of them in the oceans! They were living. So, their bodies held lots of the sun's energy. They also held energy from their food.

When they died their bodies sank to the ocean floor. They piled up for millions of years. The piles got thicker. They got mixed. Sediments buried them. The layers of sediments and dead things made pressure. They also made things very hot.

Pressure and heat worked with each other. They changed the buried plants and animals. They were no longer solid. Now, they could flow. In time, they became petroleum and natural gas. There were movements in the earth. This pushed them closer to the surface.

Coal was made in a similar way. But it was made on land. Millions of years ago, the land was not like it is now. There were swamps over large parts of Earth. Lots of plants and animals lived there. When they died their bodies piled up on the ground. Years and years went by. More materials piled up thicker and thicker. It was all buried deep underground. This created heat and pressure. This heat and pressure changed them. They became coal and natural gas.

Many years later, humans came along. We learned how to get fossil fuels out of the ground. We learned how to use the fuels for many different things.

Think About It!

What are fossil fuels?

The Story of Fossil Fuels

What Are Fossil Fuels?

Fossil fuels are substances such as petroleum, coal, and natural gas. We use them every day. They are called fossil fuels for this reason. The fossil part is because they are made from organisms that died many years ago. They were buried under many layers of dirt and rock called *sediment*. They are fuels because they provide energy that powers most of our needs.

Petroleum is a fossil fuel. It is made from very tiny organisms. The organisms lived in the oceans long ago. Coal is made from plants and animals that lived on land. Natural gas is made in both places, in oceans and on land. But all these fuels have one thing in common. The organisms that made them lived and died hundreds of millions of years ago.

All these fuels provide most of the energy demands for the world today. Each is considered a nonrenewable resource. That means they are not easily renewed, or replenished. It will take many millions of years to renew them.

How Are Fossil Fuels Made?

Petroleum and natural gas are made from plants and animals that died hundreds of millions of years ago. Back then, very small plants and animals floated in the oceans. They were much like the ones we know now. The plants are called *phytoplankton*. They were able to use photosynthesis just like other plants. The animals are called *zooplankton*. They ate other tiny animals. They also ate living and dead plants. Though tiny, there were billions of them in the oceans. Because they were living, their bodies held lots of the sun's energy. They also held energy from food they ate.

As they died, their bodies settled on the ocean floor. They piled up for millions of years. The piles got thicker over time. They got mixed and buried by sediments. The layers of sediments and dead things made pressure. They also made things very hot.

Pressure and heat transformed the buried plants and animals. They were no longer solids, but materials that could flow. In time, they became petroleum and natural gas. Movements in the earth pushed them closer to the surface.

Coal was made in a similar way, but on land. Millions of years ago, there were swamps over large parts of Earth's surface. Lots of plants and animals lived there. As these organisms died, their bodies piled up on the ground. Years and years went by. More materials piled up thicker and thicker. Everything got buried deep underground. This created a hot, high-pressure environment. And that changed the materials into coal and natural gas.

Many years later, human beings came along. Humans learned how to get fossil fuels out of the ground. And they learned how to use the fuels for many different purposes.

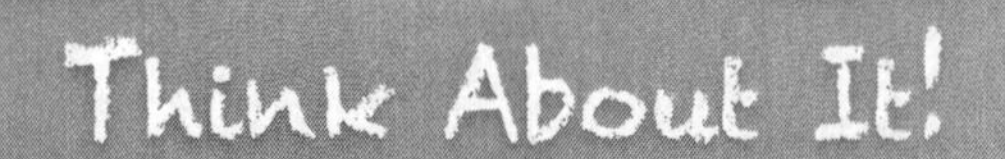

What are some possible alternatives for power since fossil fuels are nonrenewable resources?

The Story of Fossil Fuels

What Are Fossil Fuels?

Fossil fuels are substances such as petroleum, coal, and natural gas. We use them every day. They are called fossil fuels because they are made from organisms that died and were buried under many layers of dirt and rock called *sediment*. They are fuels because they provide energy that powers most of our needs today.

Petroleum is a fossil fuel that is made from very tiny organisms that lived in the oceans long ago. Coal is made from plants and animals that lived on land. Natural gas is made in both places, in oceans and on land. But all these fuels have one thing in common. The organisms that made them lived and died hundreds of millions of years ago.

All these fuels provide most of the energy demands for the world. Each is considered a nonrenewable resource, which means they are not easily renewed, or replenished. It will take many millions of years to renew them.

How Are Fossil Fuels Made?

Petroleum and natural gas are made from plants and animals that died hundreds of millions of years ago. Back then, very small plants and animals, much like the ones we know now, floated in the oceans. The plants are called *phytoplankton*, and they were capable of photosynthesis just like other plants. The animals are called *zooplankton*, and they ate other tiny animals and living and dead plants. Though minuscule, there were billions of them in the oceans. Because they were living, their bodies held a lot of the sun's energy and energy from their food.

As they died, their bodies settled on the ocean bottoms and piled up for millions of years. The piles got thicker over time and got mixed and buried by sediments. The layers of sediments and dead things made pressure and also made things very hot.

Pressure and heat transformed the buried plants and animals until they were no longer solid, but materials that could flow. In time, they became petroleum and natural gas. Movements in the earth pushed them closer to the surface.

Coal was made in a similar way, but on land. Millions of years ago, there were swamps over large parts of Earth's surface with many plants and animals living there. As these organisms died, their bodies piled up on the ground. Years and years went by and more materials piled up thicker and thicker. Everything got buried deep underground. This created a hot, high-pressure environment. That changed the materials into coal and natural gas.

Many years later, human beings came along. Humans learned how to get fossil fuels out of the ground and how to use the fuels for many different purposes.

What changes would you suggest we make in the world to help conserve our fossil fuels?

Pocahontas

Who Was Pocahontas?

Around 1595, a baby girl was born. She was an American Indian. Her name was Matoaka. This means "Little Snow Feather." Her father, the chief Powhatan, gave her a nickname. It was Pocahontas. This means "Playful One." She had tons of energy. She loved playing outdoors. Her family lived in the Chesapeake Bay region. She ate oysters and fish. She lived by the forest. It was home to deer, beavers, and wild turkeys.

In 1607, Pocahontas saw something new. She saw British settlers! The American Indians called them white men. This was because of their pale skin. Pocahontas loved to hear stories of the white men. They came on large ships. They lived in a place called Fort James. The fort was named after King James I of England. Later, the fort's name was changed to Jamestown.

The American Indians watched the settlers in secret. They hid in tall grass around the fort. The settlers looked strange to them. The white men had more hair than they did. And the white settlers wore funny-looking clothes. All of the things about them seemed odd.

Pocahontas Kidnapped!

By 1613, there was a problem. The British and the American Indians were not getting along. Captain Argall had an idea. He would kidnap Pocahontas! She was the chief's daughter. Argall thought this would make the chief do what they wanted. Argall tricked Pocahontas. She came on his ship. The captain wanted two things from Chief Powhatan. He wanted British prisoners set free. And he wanted the American Indians to give up their guns.

Argall wanted the chief to agree. Then he would send Pocahontas home. But the chief did not agree. He only sent back some of the men. The guns he returned did not work. He asked the settlers to take care of his daughter. She was still a captive!

illustration of Pocahontas

Life as a Captive

Argall took Pocahontas to a farm in Henrico, Virginia. This is near Richmond. He was afraid to stay. He thought her tribe would attack to get her back. She was taught the Christian faith. She was the first Indian convert. They gave her a new name, Rebecca.

Rebecca had to get rid of her deerskin clothes. She learned English. She prayed to their God. She was a bright student. Rebecca dressed like her captors. She acted and prayed like them, too. They became her friends.

Being a captive changed her life. Rebecca fell in love with a man. His name was John Rolfe. She got to see her father once more. She told him she loved Rolfe. Her father gave his blessing. She was married on April 5, 1614. There was peace once again between the American Indians and the settlers.

Pocahontas (Lady Rebecca) in traditional Western attire

Think About It!

Who was Pocahontas?

Pocahontas

Who Was Pocahontas?

Around 1595, an American Indian girl was born. Her name was Matoaka. This means "Little Snow Feather." Her father, the chief Powhatan, decided to call her Pocahontas. This means "Playful One." She had tons of energy and enjoyed playing outdoors. Her family lived in the Chesapeake Bay region. She grew up eating oysters and fish. The forest where she lived was home to deer, beavers, and wild turkeys.

Pocahontas first saw British settlers in 1607. The American Indians called the settlers white men because of their pale skin. Pocahontas loved to listen to stories about the white men. The white men came on large ships. They lived in a colony called Fort James. The fort was named after King James I of England. Later, the fort's name was changed to Jamestown.

The American Indians secretly watched the settlers. They hid in tall grass around the fort. The settlers looked strange to them. The white men had more hair than they did. And the white settlers wore funny-looking clothes. Everything about them seemed odd.

Pocahontas Kidnapped!

By 1613, the British and the American Indians were no longer getting along. Captain Samuel Argall decided to kidnap Pocahontas. He thought kidnapping the chief's daughter would make him want to work with the settlers. Argall convinced someone to trick Pocahontas. She came onto his ship. The captain wanted a ransom from Chief Powhatan. He wanted British prisoners set free. And he wanted the American Indians to give up their guns.

Argall wanted the American Indians to agree. Then Pocahontas could return home. Chief Powhatan only sent back some of the prisoners. The guns he returned were broken. He asked the settlers to take care of his daughter. She remained a captive!

illustration of Pocahontas

Life as a Captive

Captain Argall took Pocahontas. They went to a farm in Henrico, Virginia. Today, this is near Richmond, Virginia. He was afraid. He thought her tribe would attack to get her back. A reverend taught her the Christian faith. She became the first American Indian convert. They gave her the name of Rebecca.

Rebecca had to get rid of her deerskin clothes. She learned English. She prayed to their God. The new convert was a bright student. Rebecca dressed, acted, and prayed like her captors. They became her friends.

The kidnapping of Pocahontas changed her life. She fell in love with a man named John Rolfe. Her captors allowed her to see her father once more. She told him she was in love with Rolfe. Chief Powhatan gave his blessing. She got married on April 5, 1614. There was peace once again between the American Indians and the settlers.

Pocahontas (Lady Rebecca) in traditional Western attire

Think About It!

How did Pocahontas change when she became a captive?

Pocahontas

Who Was Pocahontas?

Around 1595, an American Indian girl was born named Matoaka, which means "Little Snow Feather." Her father, the chief Powhatan, decided to call her Pocahontas, which means "Playful One." She had tons of energy and enjoyed playing outdoors. Her family lived in the Chesapeake Bay region. Pocahontas grew up eating oysters and fish. The forest where she lived was home to deer, beavers, and wild turkeys.

Pocahontas first saw British settlers in 1607. The American Indians called the settlers white men because of their pale skin. Pocahontas loved to listen to stories about the white men. The white men came on large ships and lived in a colony called Fort James, named after King James I of England. Later, the fort's name was changed to Jamestown.

The American Indians secretly watched the settlers by hiding in tall grass around the fort. The settlers looked strange to them. The white men had more hair than they did, and they wore funny looking clothes. Everything about them seemed different.

Pocahontas Kidnapped!

By 1613, the British and the American Indians were no longer getting along. Captain Samuel Argall decided to kidnap Pocahontas. He thought kidnapping Powhatan's daughter would make the chief want to work with the settlers. Argall convinced someone to trick Pocahontas into coming to his ship. The captain wanted a ransom from Chief Powhatan; he wanted British prisoners set free, and he wanted the American Indians to give up their guns.

If everyone agreed, then Pocahontas would be allowed to return home. Chief Powhatan only sent back some of the prisoners, and the guns he returned were broken. He asked the settlers to take care of Pocahontas. She remained a captive!

illustration of Pocahontas

Life as a Captive

Captain Argall took Pocahontas to a farm in Henrico, Virginia. Today, this is near Richmond, Virginia. He was afraid her tribe would attack them to get her back. Reverend Alexander Whitaker taught Pocahontas the Christian faith. She became the first American Indian convert. They gave her the name of Rebecca.

Rebecca had to get rid of her deerskin clothes. She learned the English language and prayed to their God. The new convert was a bright student. Rebecca dressed, acted, and prayed like her captors. Her captors became her friends.

The kidnapping of Pocahontas changed her life. She fell in love with a man named John Rolfe. Her captors allowed her to see her father once more. She told him she was in love with Rolfe. Chief Powhatan gave his blessing, and she got married on April 5, 1614. There was peace once again between the American Indians and the settlers.

Pocahontas (Lady Rebecca) in traditional Western attire

Think About It!

How was this conflict resolved? What are some other ways to have resolved the conflict between the white men and the American Indians?

Life in the Colonies

Northern Colonies

At first, New England was one large colony. Two religious groups moved there. In 1620, the Pilgrims came. They were from England. Their boat was called the *Mayflower*. They started a colony. It was called Plymouth Bay. The Puritans came in 1629. They began a colony, too. It was called Massachusetts Bay. The Pilgrims were promised land in Virginia. But, on the trip, their ship blew off course.

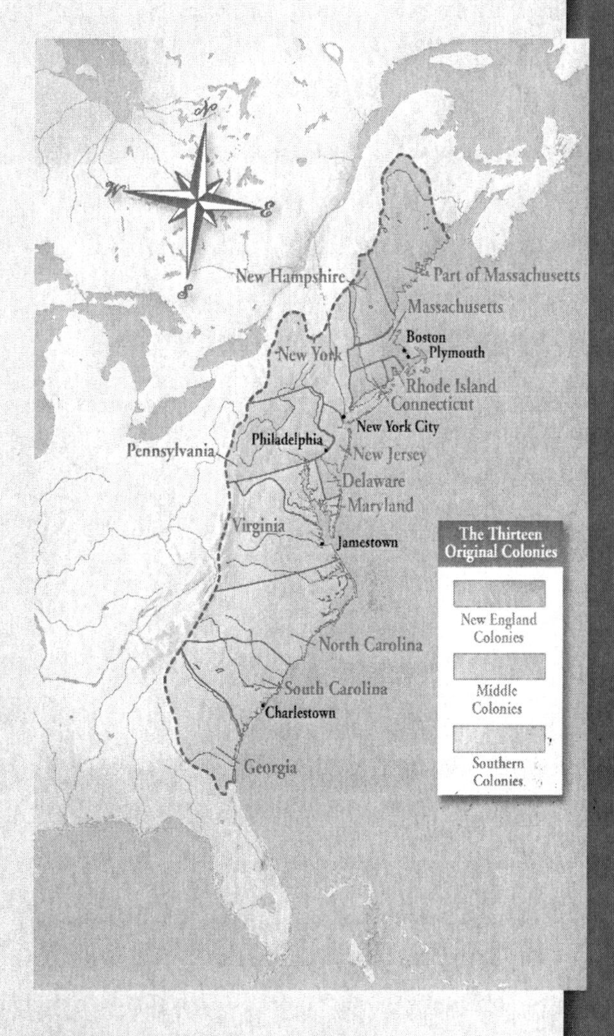

The Pilgrims learned about their new home. It was not good for farming. The soil was rocky. The winters were long. They could grow a little food. But it would only feed their families. So they had to find other ways to earn money.

In the early years, most people lived in towns. These towns were along the ocean. Certain jobs made sense. Many men built ships, traded, and fished. The forests inland had trees. They could be used for building ships. Many animals lived in the forest. They helped fur traders become rich.

Middle Colonies

The middle colonies had a name. They were called the "bread basket." They grew a lot of grain. Women used it to make breads and sweets. The colony shipped wheat, barley, and oats. They even sent livestock! They sold it to the South. They also sold it to the British West Indies.

Rivers flowed from the Appalachian Mountains to the ocean. These rivers made the land healthy. They also made it easy to trade. Farmers lived inland. But they could send their goods on the rivers. The boats took the goods. They went to the port cities of Philadelphia and New York. There, the crops could be put on large ships.

People in the middle colonies didn't just farm. They also made iron. This was a big business. Iron was used to make guns, axes, and tools.

Southern Colonies

Tobacco and rice were a big part of the Southern colonies. Indigo and corn were also. Slaves usually grew these things. They made the South successful. The land in the South was great for planting large crops. The growing season was very long. There were many rivers. This kept the soil moist and fertile.

The South was known for its large plantations farms. Plantations grow a single crop for profit. The crops raised were called *cash crops*. In Virginia, the main cash crop was tobacco. Tobacco and corn grew in the Carolinas and Maryland. In South Carolina and Georgia, rice was a cash crop. Starting in the 1740s, indigo became a cash crop for South Carolina.

Planting and tending crops took a lot of work. At first, indentured servants did the work. These men and women were very poor. They owed money because of their trips from England. They paid their debts by tending cash crops. But things had changed by the late 1600s. The plantation owners were using free slave labor from Africa.

Think About It!

Define the three colonial regions.

Life in the Colonies

Northern Colonies

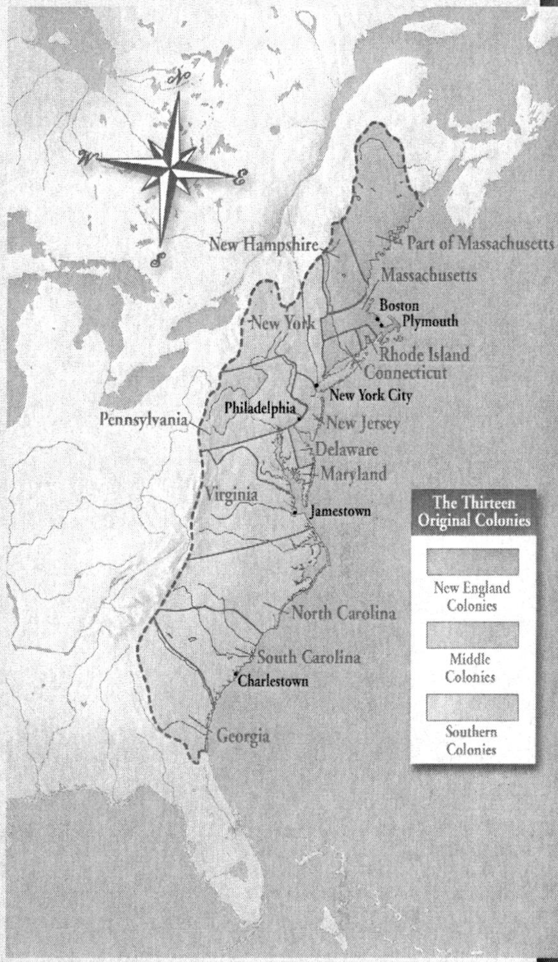

New England started as one large colony. Two religious groups settled there. In 1620, the Pilgrims came over from England. Their boat was called the *Mayflower*. They started a colony in Plymouth Bay. The Puritans came in 1629. They made the Massachusetts Bay Colony. The Pilgrims had a charter. They were promised land in Virginia. On the trip, their ship blew off course.

The Pilgrims quickly learned about their new home. It was not very good for farming. The soil was rocky. The winters were long. The Pilgrims could grow some food. But it was only enough for their families. So the colonists in New England had to find other ways to earn money.

In the early years, most colonists lived in towns along the ocean. It made sense that these men would build ships, trade, and fish. The forests inland provided trees for building ships. The many animals living in the forests helped fur traders become very rich.

Middle Colonies

The middle colonies had a nickname. They were called the "bread basket" colonies. Grain was plentiful there. Women used the grain to make breads and sweets. The colonists shipped wheat, barley, oats, and livestock. They sold it to the South and to the British West Indies.

Rivers flowed from the Appalachian Mountains to the ocean. These rivers made the land healthy. They also helped make trading very easy. Farmers who lived inland could send their goods on the rivers. The boats took the goods to the port cities of Philadelphia and New York. There, the products could be loaded onto large ships.

People in the middle colonies were also involved in manufacturing. Iron business was very important. Iron was used to make guns, axes, and tools.

Southern Colonies

Tobacco, rice, indigo, and corn were a big part of the Southern colonies. Slaves grew these crops and were one of the reasons why the South was successful. The land in the South was ideal for planting large crops. The growing season was very long. There were many rivers to keep the soil moist and fertile.

The South was famous for its large plantations. These are big farms that grow a single crop for profit. The crops raised on these farms were called *cash crops*. In Virginia, the main cash crop was tobacco. Tobacco and corn were grown in the Carolinas and Maryland. In South Carolina and Georgia, rice was a popular crop. Starting in the 1740s, indigo became a cash crop for South Carolina.

Planting crops and tending them took a lot of work. At first, the planters used indentured servants. These were men and women who were very poor. They owed money for the cost of their trips from England. So they paid it off by tending cash crops. By the late 1600s, things had changed. The plantation owners were using free slave labor from Africa.

Think About It!

What were strengths of the colonies?

Life in the Colonies

Northern Colonies

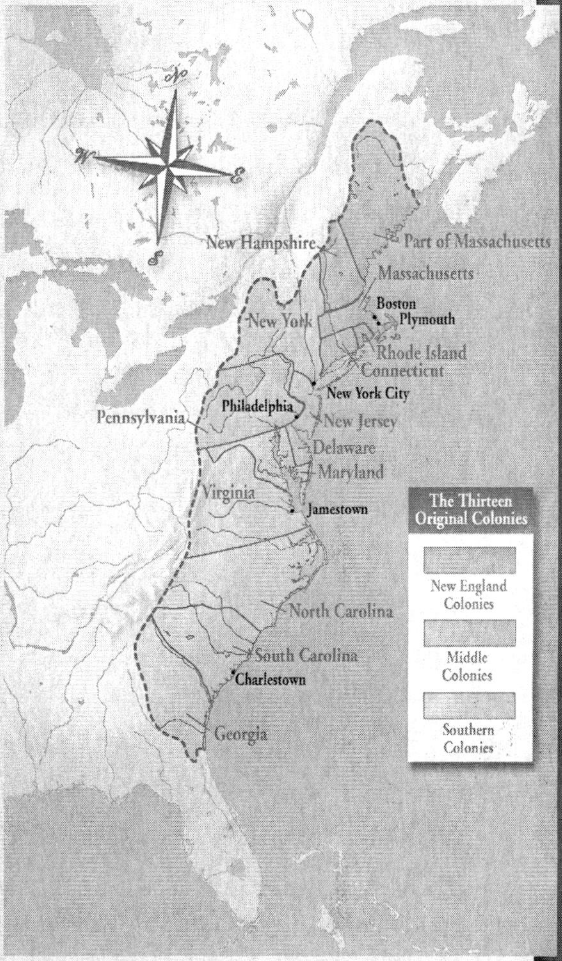

New England started as one large colony and was settled by two different religious groups. In 1620, the Pilgrims came over from England on the *Mayflower* and started a colony in Plymouth Bay. The Puritans followed in 1629 and started the successful Massachusetts Bay Colony. The Pilgrims had a charter that promised them land in Virginia. On the trip across, their ship blew off course.

The Pilgrims quickly learned that their new home was not very good for farming. The soil was rocky, and the winters were long. The Pilgrims could only grow enough food to feed their own families. So the colonists in New England had to find other ways to earn money.

In the early years, most colonists lived in towns along the ocean. It made sense that these men would become shipbuilders, traders, and fishermen. The forests inland provided trees for building ships. The many animals living in the forests helped fur traders become very rich.

Middle Colonies

The middle colonies were called the "bread basket" colonies because grain was plentiful. Women used the grain to make breads and sweets. The colonists exported wheat, barley, oats, and livestock to the South and to the British West Indies.

Rivers flowed from the Appalachian Mountains to the ocean. These rivers made the land healthy. They also helped make trading very easy. Farmers who lived inland could send their goods on the rivers. The boats took the goods to the port cities of Philadelphia and New York. There, the products could be loaded onto large ships.

People in the middle colonies were involved in manufacturing. The iron industry was important because iron was used to make guns, axes, and tools.

Southern Colonies

Tobacco, rice, indigo, and corn were grown in Southern colonies. Slaves grew these crops, and they were a large part of what made the Southern colonies successful. The land in the South was ideal for planting large crops. Because of the warm climate, the growing season was very long. There were many rivers to keep the soil moist and fertile.

The South was famous for its large plantations. A plantation is a big farm that produces a single crop for profit. The crops raised on plantations were called *cash crops*. In Virginia, the main cash crop was tobacco. Tobacco and corn were produced in the Carolinas and Maryland. In South Carolina and Georgia, rice was a profitable crop. Starting in the 1740s, indigo became a cash crop for South Carolina.

Planting crops and tending them took a lot of work. At first, the planters used indentured servants. These were men and women who were very poor. They paid off the cost of their trips from England by working in the colonies. By the late 1600s, the plantation owners were using free slave labor from Africa.

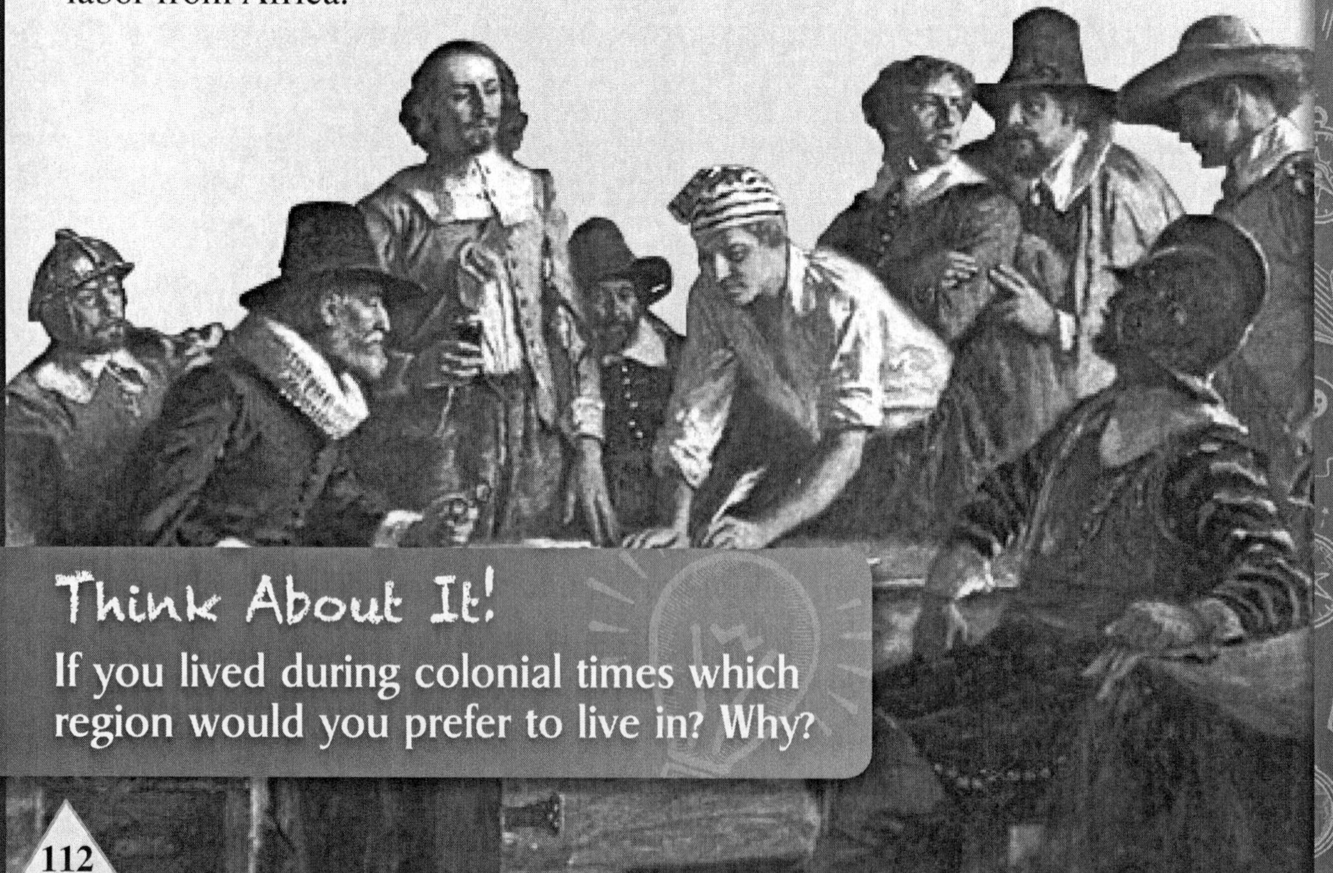

Think About It!

If you lived during colonial times which region would you prefer to live in? Why?

Marie Antoinette

Powerful Teen Queen

Marie Antoinette was young when she married. She was only 14 years old! She married Louis XVI. He was the grandson of the king of France. King Louis XV died from small pox in 1774. The couple found out the king died. They wept. Louis XVI became king. That made Marie Antoinette the queen of France. She was only 18. They felt they were too young to rule France.

Marie Antoinette

At first, Marie was popular with the French people. Louis XV had been king for a long time. People were unhappy with him. They were pleased to have a new royal couple in power. They liked Marie. She was pretty and charming.

It did not take Marie long to enjoy her new role. She quickly used her power. She changed old customs in the French court. She stopped eating in public. She dressed in private. She also fired some of the servants. Marie may have felt she was making things better. But she also made mistakes. She was not polite to older women at court. Marie had only been queen for a month. The French court began to turn against her.

A Life of Luxury

As queen, Marie Antoinette did not think about her subjects' needs. Instead, she focused on having fun. She lived a life of luxury. She liked the opera, theater, and costume balls. She used France's money. She spent lots of money on dresses and jewelry. Soon, Marie was known as the Queen of Fashion.

Marie had a new frivolous lifestyle. It upset the large peasant class in France. These farmers and workers no longer liked the young queen. They resented her. They did not like her selfish spending habits. They quickly lost hope. She would not help improve their lives.

Marie lived at the Palace of Versailles. She was far removed from normal life in France. Louis XVI and Marie had visited Paris. This was before they became king and queen. The city was cleaned before they came. Smelly mud in the streets was carted away. Beggars were kept out of sight. Marie did not know how the French people really lived. She later learned the people were angry with her. This surprised her.

A Mother at Last

In 1778, Marie Antoinette finally had her first child. The baby was a girl. She had her first son in 1781. Her second son was born in 1785. Marie was more mature after she had children. She settled down. She spent time with them.

Having children should have helped Marie's status. She had done her duty. She had given birth to an heir. But the people of France still had doubts about Marie. They kept looking for reasons not to like her. Marie may have changed. But many of her subjects did not. They wouldn't change their minds about her. They wanted to believe the worst.

Think About It!

What made the people of France turn against their queen?

Marie Antoinette

Powerful Teen Queen

Marie Antoinette was 14 years old when she married Louis XVI. He was the grandson of the king of France, King Louis XV. The king died from small pox in 1774. When the couple found out the king died they wept. Louis XVI became king. That made Marie Antoinette the queen of France. She was only 18. The new king and queen felt they were too young to rule France.

Marie Antoinette

Marie was popular with the French people when she first became queen. They had been unhappy with Louis XV in his later years. They were pleased to have a new royal couple in power. And they liked Marie. She was pretty and charming.

It did not take Marie Antoinette long to begin enjoying her new role. She quickly used her power to change old customs in the French court. She stopped eating in public and dressed in private. She dismissed some of the servants. Marie may have felt she was making improvements. But she also made mistakes. She was disrespectful to the older women at court. Within a month of her reign, the French court began to turn against Marie Antoinette.

A Life of Luxury

As queen, Marie Antoinette did not think about her subjects' needs. Instead, she focused on enjoying herself and living a life of luxury. She liked the opera, theater, and costume balls. She used France's money and spent it on dresses and jewelry. Soon, Marie was known as the Queen of Fashion.

Marie Antoinette's new frivolous lifestyle offended the large peasant class in France. These farmers and laborers no longer liked the young queen. They resented her and her thoughtless spending habits. They quickly lost hope that she would make changes that would help improve their lives.

At the Palace of Versailles, Marie Antoinette was far removed from normal life in France. Before Louis XVI and Marie became king and queen, they had visited Paris. The city was cleaned before their visit. Smelly mud that collected in the streets was carted away. Beggars were kept out of sight. Marie did not know how the French people really lived. She was surprised when she later learned the French people were angry with her.

A Mother at Last

In 1778, Marie Antoinette finally gave birth to her first child, a girl. She had her first son in 1781 and her second son in 1785. Marie grew more mature after she had children. She settled down. She spent time with her children.

Having children should have helped Marie's reputation. She had fulfilled her duty. She had produced an heir. However, the people of France were still suspicious of Marie. They continued to look for reasons to dislike her. Marie Antoinette may have changed. But many of her subjects would not change their minds about her. They wanted to believe the worst.

Think About It!

Why do you think having children made Marie change her ways?

Marie Antoinette

Powerful Teen Queen

Marie Antoinette was 14 years old when she married Louis XVI. He was the grandson of the king of France, King Louis XV. The king died from small pox in 1774. When the couple found out the king died, they wept. Louis XVI became the new king of France, which made Marie Antoinette the queen. She was only 18 at the time. The new king and queen felt they were too young to rule France.

Marie Antoinette

Marie Antoinette was popular with the French people when she first became queen. They had been unhappy with Louis XV in his later years and were pleased to have a new royal couple in power. And they liked Marie Antoinette because she was beautiful and charming.

It did not take Marie Antoinette long to begin enjoying her new role. She quickly used her power to change old customs in the French court. She stopped eating in public and began dressing in private. She also dismissed some of the servants who worked for her. Marie Antoinette may have felt she was making improvements, but she also made mistakes. She was disrespectful to the older women at court. Within a month of her reign, the French court began to turn against Marie Antoinette.

A Life of Luxury

As queen, Marie Antoinette did not think about her subjects' needs. Instead, she focused on enjoying herself and living a life of luxury. She liked the opera, theater, and masquerade balls. She used France's money on dresses and jewelry. Soon, Antoinette was known as the Queen of Fashion.

Marie Antoinette's new frivolous lifestyle offended the large peasant class in France. These farmers and laborers no longer liked the young queen. They resented her and her thoughtless spending habits. They quickly lost hope that she would make changes that would help improve their lives.

At the Palace of Versailles, Marie Antoinette was far removed from normal life in France. Before Louis XVI and Marie Antoinette became king and queen, they had visited Paris. But the city was cleaned before their visit. Smelly mud that collected in the streets was carted away, and beggars were kept out of sight. Marie Antoinette did not know how the French people really lived. She was surprised when she later learned the French people were angry with her.

A Mother at Last

In 1778, Marie Antoinette finally gave birth to her first child, a girl. She had her first son in 1781 and her second son in 1785. Marie Antoinette grew more mature after she had children. She settled down and spent time with her children.

Having children should have helped Marie Antoinette's reputation. She had fulfilled her duty and produced an heir. However, the people of France were still suspicious of Marie Antoinette. They continued to look for reasons to dislike her. Marie Antoinette may have changed, but many of her subjects were unwilling to change their minds about her. They wanted to believe the worst.

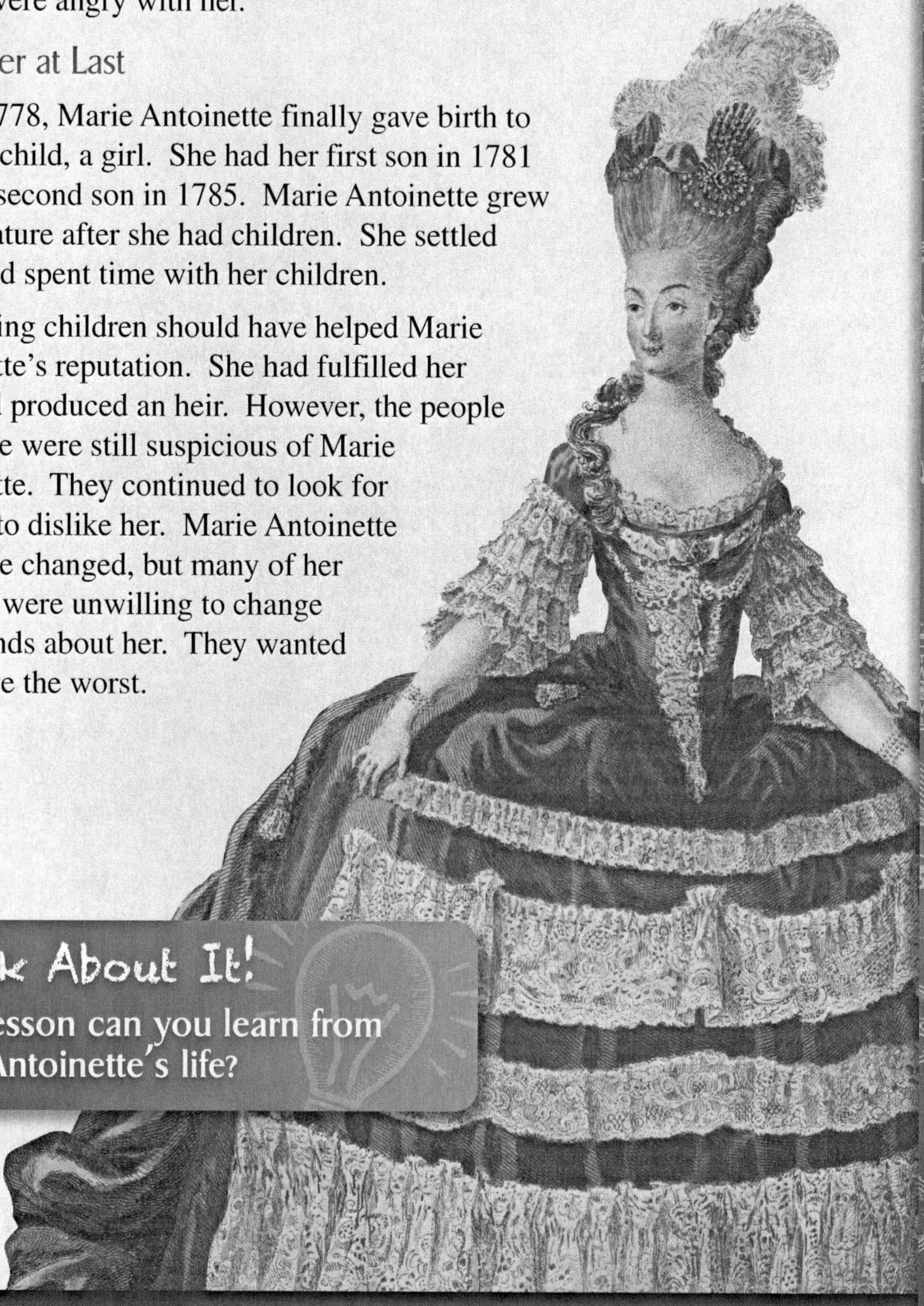

Think About It!

What lesson can you learn from Marie Antoinette's life?

Lewis and Clark

America Doubles in Size

Thomas Jefferson was the third president of the United States. It was much smaller than it is now. It did not have land west of the Mississippi River. Jefferson wanted to make the United States bigger. He had a dream. He wanted the country to stretch from ocean to ocean. In 1803, part of this dream came true.

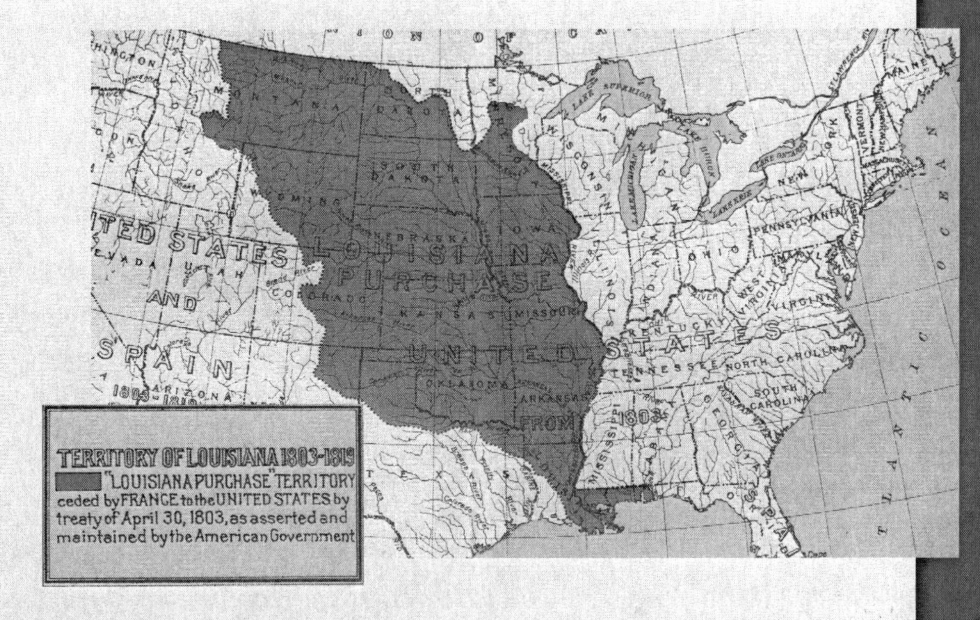

At the time, France had a leader named Napoleon Bonaparte. France had a huge area of land in the West. It was called Louisiana. Napoleon sold it to the United States. The purchase cost 15 million dollars. The country got almost 828,000 square miles (2 million square kilometers) of new land.

This was a fast change. Now America was twice as big! Jefferson wanted to know all about the new lands. He hired a group of men. The men would go on an expedition. They would travel through the new lands. Then, they would come home. They would tell about the things they saw.

Preparing for the Journey

Jefferson knew who should lead the trip. He had known Meriwether Lewis all his life. They were neighbors in Virginia. For a while, Lewis was in the army. Now, he worked for Jefferson. He was his secretary. Lewis was brave, strong, and curious. Lewis was glad to take the job. He started choosing the rest of his crew. First, he asked his friend William Clark to be his co-captain. Clark was from Kentucky. He had been in the army with Lewis. He had a lot of skills. He had traveled in the wild. He knew how to travel on rivers and lakes.

Lewis did a lot of work to get ready for the trip. Five scientists taught him new things for the trip. He learned about plants and animals. He studied navigation and surveying. And he even learned American Indian history! Lewis was told what supplies to bring. He went to St. Louis in the winter of 1803–04. His crew of about 40 men met him there. Lewis called them the Corps of Discovery. The men set up camp. Then they spent months training. They built boats. They exercised and practiced shooting.

Finally Underway in May

The Corps began its trip on May 14, 1804. The men left in three boats. One was a large wooden keelboat. It took 21 men to row it. The other two were different. They were small boats called *pirogues* (PEE-rohgs). The men planned to travel northwest. They would go along the Missouri River. This would lead them to the Rocky Mountains. There, they would cross a pass to get through them. There were rivers on the other side. These would take them to the Pacific Ocean.

Lewis was a good leader. The men respected him. They trusted him. But he was very serious. He liked to be alone. Clark was more fun. He loved to talk and told jokes. Clark was in charge of the boats. Each captain kept a journal during the trip. They wrote about what happened. They described the weather. They made maps of the land and the water. They drew all the new plants and animals they saw. These included bison and coyotes. They also saw prairie dogs and jackrabbits.

Lewis and Clark

Think About It!

How did the Corps prepare for their trip?

Lewis and Clark

America Doubles in Size

Thomas Jefferson was the third president of the United States. The country was much smaller than it is today. America did not have any land west of the Mississippi River. Jefferson wanted to make the United States bigger. He dreamed the country would stretch across the continent. In 1803, part of this dream came true.

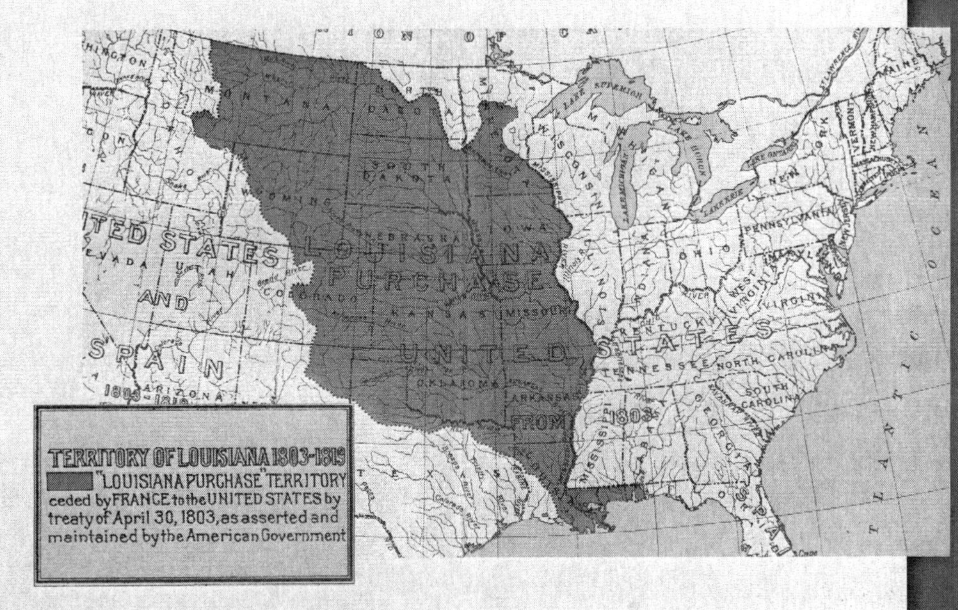

At that time, France had a very powerful leader. His name was Napoleon Bonaparte. France had a huge area of land in the West. The land was called Louisiana. Napoleon sold it to the United States. The Louisiana Purchase cost 15 million dollars. For that, the country got almost 828,000 square miles (2 million square kilometers) of new land.

All of a sudden, America was twice as big! Jefferson wanted to know all about the new lands. He decided to send a group of men on an expedition. They would travel through the Louisiana Territory. Then, they would come home and tell about everything they saw.

Preparing for the Journey

Jefferson knew who he wanted to lead the trip. He had known Meriwether Lewis all his life. Their families were neighbors in Virginia. For a while, Lewis was in the army. Now, he was Jefferson's personal secretary. Lewis was brave, strong, and curious. He was happy to take the job. He started choosing the rest of his crew. First, he asked an old army friend to be his co-captain. William Clark was from Kentucky. He had a lot of experience. He had traveled in the wild and along rivers and lakes.

Lewis did a lot of studying to get ready for the trip. Five different scientists taught him new things for the journey. He learned about plants and animals. He studied navigation and surveying. He learned American Indian history, too! The scientists also told Lewis what supplies to bring. Lewis traveled to St. Louis in the winter of 1803–04. His crew of about 40 men met him there. Lewis called them the Corps of Discovery. The men set up camp. Then, they spent months training. They built boats, exercised, and practiced shooting.

Finally Underway in May

The Corps of Discovery began its journey on May 14, 1804. The men left in three boats. One was a large wooden keelboat. It took 21 men to row it. The other two were smaller boats called *pirogues* (PEE-rohgs). They planned to travel northwest along the Missouri River. This would lead them to the Rocky Mountains. There, they would cross a pass through the mountains. Rivers on the other side would take them to the Pacific Ocean.

Lewis was a good leader. The men respected and trusted him. But he was very serious and liked to be alone. Clark was more fun. He loved to talk and tell jokes. He was in charge of the boats. Each of the captains kept a journal during their travels. They wrote about their adventures. They wrote down the weather. They made maps of the land and the water. They drew and described all the new plants and animals they saw. These included bison, coyotes, prairie dogs, and jackrabbits.

Lewis and Clark

Think About It!

Why did the group prepare for the trip by building boats, exercising, and practicing shooting?

Lewis and Clark

America Doubles in Size

Thomas Jefferson became the third president of the United States in 1801. The country was much smaller than it is today. America did not have any land west of the Mississippi River. Jefferson wanted to make the United States bigger and dreamed of the country reaching across the continent. In 1803, part of this dream came true.

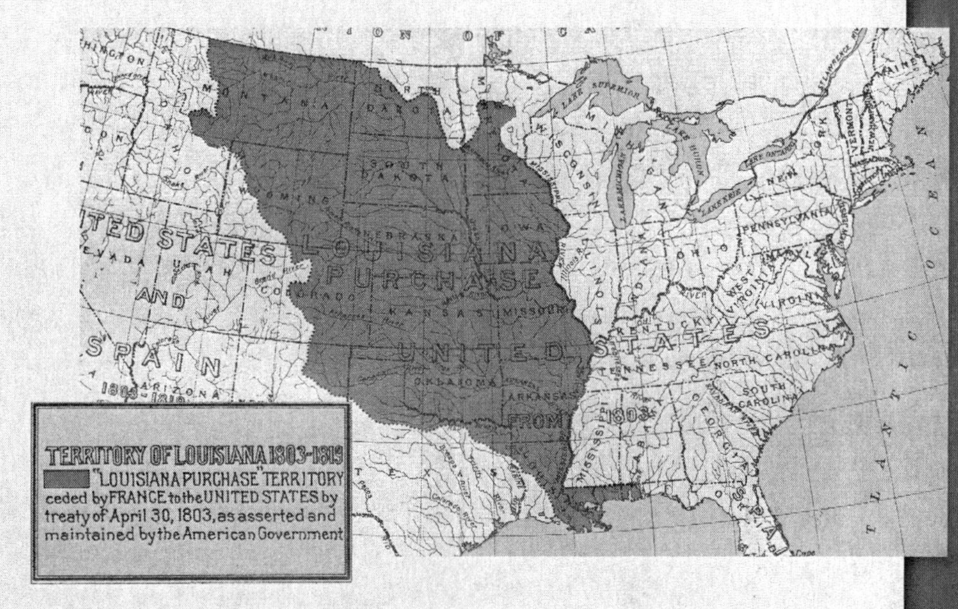

France had a very powerful leader named Napoleon Bonaparte. France had a huge area of land in the West called Louisiana. Napoleon offered to sell it to the United States. The Louisiana Purchase cost America 15 million dollars. For that, the country got almost 828,000 square miles (2 million square kilometers) of new land for the growing country.

All of a sudden, America was twice as big! Jefferson wanted to know all about America's new lands, so he decided to send a group of men on an expedition. They would travel through the Louisiana Territory. Then they would come home and tell about everything they saw.

Preparing for the Journey

Jefferson knew just who he wanted to lead the trip. He had known Meriwether Lewis all his life. Their families were neighbors in Virginia. For a while, Lewis was in the army, but now he was Jefferson's personal secretary. Jefferson knew Lewis was brave, strong, and curious. Lewis was happy to take the job. He started choosing the rest of his crew. First, he asked an old army friend to be his co-captain. William Clark was from Kentucky and had a lot of experience traveling in the wilderness and along rivers and lakes.

Lewis did a lot of studying to get ready for the expedition. Five different scientists taught him important things for the journey. He learned about plants and animals. He studied navigation, surveying, and American Indian history. The scientists also told Lewis what supplies to bring. Lewis traveled to St. Louis in the winter of 1803–04, and his crew of about 40 men met him there. Lewis called them the Corps of Discovery. The men set up camp and spent months training. They built boats, exercised, and practiced shooting.

Finally Underway in May

The Corps of Discovery began its journey on May 14, 1804. The men left in three boats. One was a large wooden keelboat that took 21 men to row it. The other two were smaller boats called *pirogues* (PEE-rohgs). They planned to travel northwest along the Missouri River. This would lead them to the Rocky Mountains, where they would cross a pass through the mountains. Rivers on the other side would take them to the Pacific Ocean.

Lewis and Clark

Lewis was a good leader. The men respected and trusted him, but he was very serious and liked to be alone. Clark was more fun. He loved to talk and tell jokes. He was in charge of the boats. Both captains kept journals during the expedition and wrote about their adventures. They recorded the weather and made maps of the land and the water. They drew and described all the new plants and animals they saw. These included bison, coyotes, prairie dogs, and jackrabbits.

Think About It!

What are some obstacles that Lewis and Clark may have encountered on their voyage?

Dr. Martin Luther King Jr.

The Dreamer

The world is full of dreamers. One dreamer was Dr. Martin Luther King Jr. When he was young, he had an idea. He told his mom he would turn this world upside down. This first dream came true. At that age, he did not know he would be a leader. In fact, he would lead the United States's second civil war. It is sure that King had many more dreams. But one stood out from the rest. He said he had a dream. He wanted his four little children to live in a place where, "they will not be judged by the color of their skin but instead by the content of their character."

King grew up during a very hard time in the South. The South had laws that kept races apart from each other. African Americans and white people were separate. They could not go to the same places to eat. They couldn't drink from the same fountains. This is called *segregation*.

The Battle for Birmingham

Birmingham is a city in Alabama. It was a segregated city. King knew he had to go there. He planned to protest at clothing stores. The stores wanted African Americans to shop there. But the stores' owners did not allow them to use the restrooms. And they could not eat at the lunch counters.

King showed up in old clothes. He wanted to show that he would rather wear old work clothes. He did not want to shop for nice clothes at these stores. He called the plan Project C. The C stood for confrontation. His protest was peaceful. But he hoped the store owners would react in a bad way. Then the media would report it. That would make people notice what was going on.

Many African Americans lived in Birmingham. They did not want to get involved. Some were middle-class citizens. They did not want to give up what they had worked so hard to achieve. Others knew they would lose their jobs if they joined the protest. King was arrested. That got the media's attention!

A Letter from Jail

King's time in jail was hard. At first, police placed King all alone in a narrow cell. It did not have a mattress. He knew his friends had run out of bail money. To top it off, there were eight white ministers in the town. They wrote a statement for the local paper. In this statement, they urged African Americans to stop their protest.

King felt he must respond to this statement. But he had nothing to write with in jail. So, over a couple of days, his lawyer snuck in a pen and paper. King wrote a response letter. He explained why African Americans had to protest. He said the only way to spur change was to bring attention to it. Having a protest does this. Only then will people see that change is needed.

His arrest got the attention King wanted. More than 1,000 children and young adults joined together. They met at a church. They held a peaceful meeting. But the police brought dogs to attack them and fire hoses to spray them. The media caught this on tape. The nation watched these awful events in horror. Through peaceful actions, King got the nation to focus on the civil rights problems.

civil rights protest

Think About It!

Describe how Dr. King fought for equal rights.

Dr. Martin Luther King Jr.

The Dreamer

If ever there was a dreamer, it was Dr. Martin Luther King Jr. When he was just a little kid, he told his mother he was going to turn this world upside down. There is no denying that this first dream came true. At that age, he had no idea he would fight his nation's second civil war. It is certain that King had many more dreams. But there was one that stood out from the rest. He said, "I have a dream that my four little children will one day live in a nation where they will not be judged by the color of their skin but by the content of their character."

King grew up during a very difficult time in the South. The South had laws that kept races separate from one another. African Americans and white people could not go to the same restaurants or drink from the same fountains. This treatment is called *segregation*.

The Battle for Birmingham

Birmingham was a segregated city in Alabama. King knew he had to go there. He planned to protest at clothing stores. The stores wanted African Americans to shop there. But African Americans were not allowed to use the stores' restrooms. And they could not eat at the lunch counters.

King showed up in old clothes. He wanted to show that he would rather wear old work clothes than shop for nice clothes at these stores. He called the plan Project C. The C stood for confrontation. He hoped to get the store owners to react in a bad way to his peaceful protest. Then, the media would report it. That would make people notice what was going on.

Many African Americans in Birmingham did not want to get involved. Some were middle-class citizens. They did not want to give up what they had worked so hard to achieve. Others knew they would lose their jobs if they joined in the protest. King ended up being arrested. That got the media's attention!

A Letter from Jail

King's time in the Birmingham jail was hard. At first, police placed King all alone in a narrow cell that did not have a mattress. He knew his supporters had run out of bail money. To top it off, eight white ministers in the town wrote a statement for the local paper. In this statement, they urged African Americans to stop protesting.

King felt that he must respond to this statement. He had nothing to write with in jail. So, over a couple of days, his lawyer smuggled in a pen and paper. In his response letter, King explained why African Americans had to protest. He said that the only way to spur change was to bring attention to it. Protesting does this. Only then will people see that change is needed.

His arrest got the attention King wanted. More than 1,000 children and young adults joined together at a church. They held a peaceful meeting. Unfortunately, the police brought in dogs to attack them and fire hoses to spray them. The media caught this on tape, and the nation watched these terrible events in horror. Through peaceful actions, King got the nation's attention focused on the civil rights problems.

civil rights protest

Think About It!

Why did Dr. King insist on peaceful protests?

Dr. Martin Luther King Jr.

The Dreamer

If ever there was a dreamer, it was Dr. Martin Luther King Jr. When he was just a little kid, he told his mother he was going to turn this world upside down. There is no denying that this first dream came true. At that age, he had no idea he would fight his nation's second civil war. It is certain that King had many more dreams, but there was one that stood out from the rest. He said, "I have a dream that my four little children will one day live in a nation where they will not be judged by the color of their skin but by the content of their character."

King grew up during a very difficult time in the South because the South had laws that kept races separate from one another. African Americans and whites people could not go to the same restaurants or drink from the same water fountains. This treatment is called *segregation*.

The Battle for Birmingham

Birmingham, Alabama, was a segregated city, and King knew he had to go there. He planned to protest at department stores. The stores wanted African Americans to shop there, but African Americans were not allowed to use the stores' restrooms or eat at the lunch counters.

King showed up in old clothes because he wanted to show he would rather wear old work clothes than shop for nice clothes at these stores. He called the plan Project C; the C stood for confrontation. He hoped to get the store owners to react in a bad way to his peaceful protest so the media would report it. That would bring attention to what was happening.

Many African Americans in Birmingham did not want to get involved. Some were middle-class citizens and did not want to give up what they had worked so hard to achieve. Others knew they would lose their jobs if they joined in the protest. King ended up being arrested at the protest, which got the media's attention!

A Letter from Jail

King's time in the Birmingham jail was hard. At first, police placed King all alone in a narrow cell that did not have a mattress. He knew his supporters had run out of bail money. To make matters worse, eight white ministers in the town wrote a statement for the local paper urging African Americans to stop protesting.

King felt that he must respond to this statement, but he had nothing to write with in jail. So, over a couple of days, his lawyer smuggled in a pen and paper. In his response letter, King explained why African Americans had to protest. He said the only way to spur change was to bring attention to it and protesting accomplishes this. Only then will people see that change is necessary.

His arrest got the attention King wanted. More than 1,000 children and young adults joined together at a church and held a peaceful meeting. Unfortunately, the police brought in dogs to attack them and fire hoses to spray them. The media caught this on tape, and the nation watched these terrible events in horror. Through peaceful actions, King got the nation's attention focused on the civil rights problems.

civil rights protest

Think About It!

How did the negative reactions to Dr. King help the Civil Rights Movement?

References Cited

August, Diane, and Timothy Shanahan. 2006. *Developing Literacy in Second-Language Learners: Report of the National Literacy Panel on Language-Minority Children and Youth.* Mahwah, New Jersey: Lawrence Erlbaum Associates, Inc.

Fountas, Irene, and Gay Su Pinnell. 2012. *The Critical Role of Text Complexity in Teaching Children to Read.* Portsmouth, Virginia: Heinemann.

Tomlinson, Carol Ann. 2014. *The Differentiated Classroom. Responding to the Needs of All Learners, 2nd Edition.* Reston, Virginia: Association for Supervision and Curriculum Development.

Van Tassel-Baska, Joyce. 2003. "Differentiating the Language Arts for High Ability Learners, K–8. ERIC Digest." Arlington, Virginia: ERIC Clearinghouse on Disabilities and Gifted Education.

Vygotsky, Lev Semenovich. 1978. "Interaction Between Learning and Development." In *Mind in Society*, 79–91. Cambridge, Massachusetts: Harvard University Press.

Strategies for Using the Leveled Texts

Throughout this section are differentiation strategies that can be used with each leveled text to support reading comprehension for the students in your classroom.

Below-Grade-Level Students

KWL Charts

KWL charts empower students to take ownership of their learning. This strategy can be used as a pre- or post-reading organizer and a tool for further exploration or research on a topic. Guide students with the following questions:

- What can scanning the text tell you about the text?
- What do you know about the topic of this text?
- What do you want to know about this text?
- What did you learn about the topic?
- What do you still want to know about the topic? (*extension question*)

What do you KNOW?	What do you WANT to know?	What did you LEARN?

Strategies for Using the Leveled Texts *(cont.)*

Below-Grade-Level Students *(cont.)*

Vocabulary Scavenger Hunt

Another prereading strategy is a Vocabulary Scavenger Hunt. Students preview the text and highlight unknown words. Students then write the words on specially divided pages. The pages are divided into quarters with the following headings: *Definition*, *Sentence*, *Examples*, and *Nonexamples*. A section called *Picture* is put over the middle of the chart. As an alternative, teachers can give students selected words from the text and have them fill in the chart individually. (Sample words can be found on page 134).

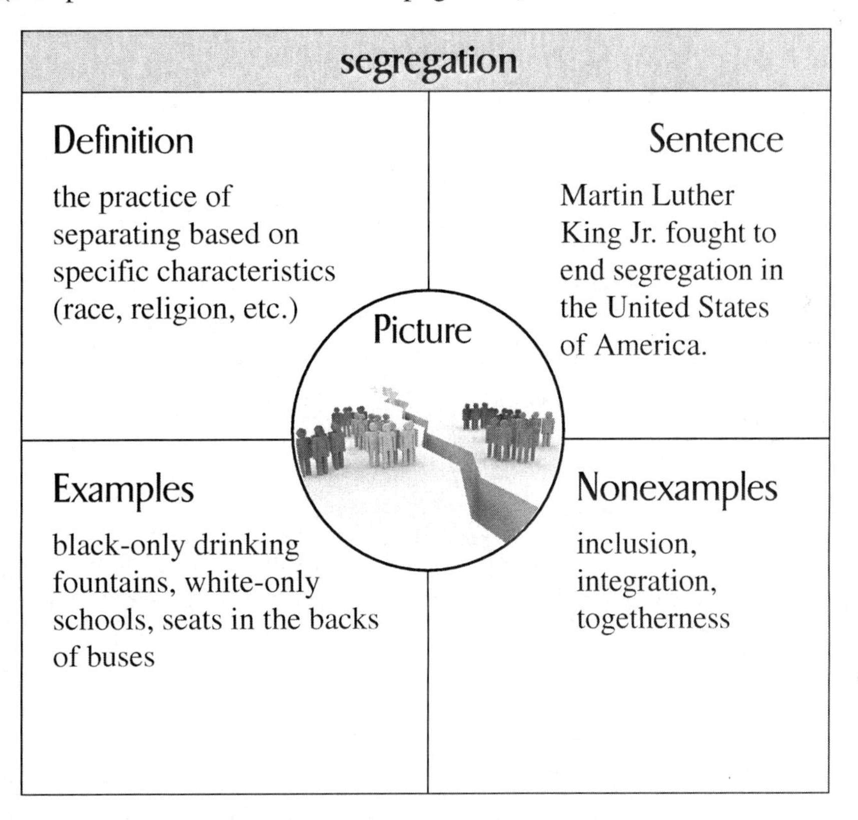

This encounter with new vocabulary words enables students to use the words properly. The definition identifies the word's meaning in student-friendly language, which can be constructed by the teacher and/or student. The sentence should be written so that the word is used in context. This sentence can be either one students make up or copied from the text in which the word is found. This helps students make connections with background knowledge. Illustrating the word gives a visual clue. Examples help students prepare for factual questions from the teacher or on standardized assessments. Nonexamples help students prepare for *not* and *except for* test questions such as "All of these are examples of segregation *except for* . . ." and "Which of these examples are *not* segregation?" Any information students are not able to record before reading can be added after reading the text.

Strategies for Using the Leveled Texts *(cont.)*

Below-Grade-Level Students *(cont.)*

Frontloading Vocabulary and Content

As an alternative to the Vocabulary Scavenger Hunt, teachers can frontload, or pre-teach, vocabulary or content in a text prior to reading. This can be a useful tool for all students, especially below-grade-level students, who struggle with on-demand reading and comprehension tasks. Activate students' prior knowledge by asking:

- What do you know about the word/topic . . .
- All these words are about the text you are going to read. Based on these words, what do you think the text will be about?

The words below can be used during frontloading discussions before reading a text. (Note: Some words are not found in all levels but can be used to focus students' attention toward the theme and main idea of text they will read.)

Text	Words, Themes, and Content
Excerpt from *Anne of Green Gables*	grimly, despairing, obedience, suspiciously, ghastly, utterly, wretched, ashamed, astonished, grotesque, significance
Excerpt from *The Story of Dr. Dolittle*	mantel, presently, spectacles, two pence, measles, blustery, epidemic, genuine
History's Mysteries	vanished, magnetic field, historian, detective
Go-Kart Racing	blueprint, calculations, pressure, friction, estimates, gravity
Food Groups	glucose, proteins, carbohydrates, amino acids, vegetarians, vitamins, minerals, calcium
Eco-Predictions	predictions, ecosystem, pollution, data, diagram, record
Journeys: Land, Air, Sea	transportation, satellites, landmarks, drawn to scale
Patterns Around Us	geometric, tessellations, polygons
All About Sharks	predators, meters, kilograms, prey
The Bread Book	distribution, grams, kernels, dozen, mill
Producers and Consumers	producer, consumer, fuel, nutrients, herbivores, carnivores, omnivores
The Nutrient Cycle	nutrient, cycle, nitrogen, ammonia, nitrates, chlorophyll, decomposers, fungi, bacteria, oxygen, glucose, carbon, photosynthesis
Circuits	circuit, series, parallel, physics, complex circuits, resistor
Sound Waves and Communication	sound waves, pressure, vibrations, molecules, frequency, Doppler effect
The Story of Fossil Fuels	fossil fuels, coal, petroleum, sediment
Pocahontas	settlers, captive, conflict
Life in the Colonies	colonies, Pilgrims, plantations, crops
Marie Antoinette	throne, luxury, French court, subjects
Lewis and Clark	continent, Louisiana Purchase, pirogues, expedition
Dr. Martin Luther King Jr.	segregation, confrontation, middle-class, ministers, civil rights

Strategies for Using the Leveled Texts *(cont.)*

Below-Grade-Level Students *(cont.)*

Graphic Organizers to Find Similarities and Differences

Setting a purpose for reading content focuses the learner. One purpose for reading can be to identify similarities and differences. This skill must be directly taught, modeled, and applied. Many of the comprehension questions in this book ask students to compare and contrast. The chart below can be used to respond to these questions.

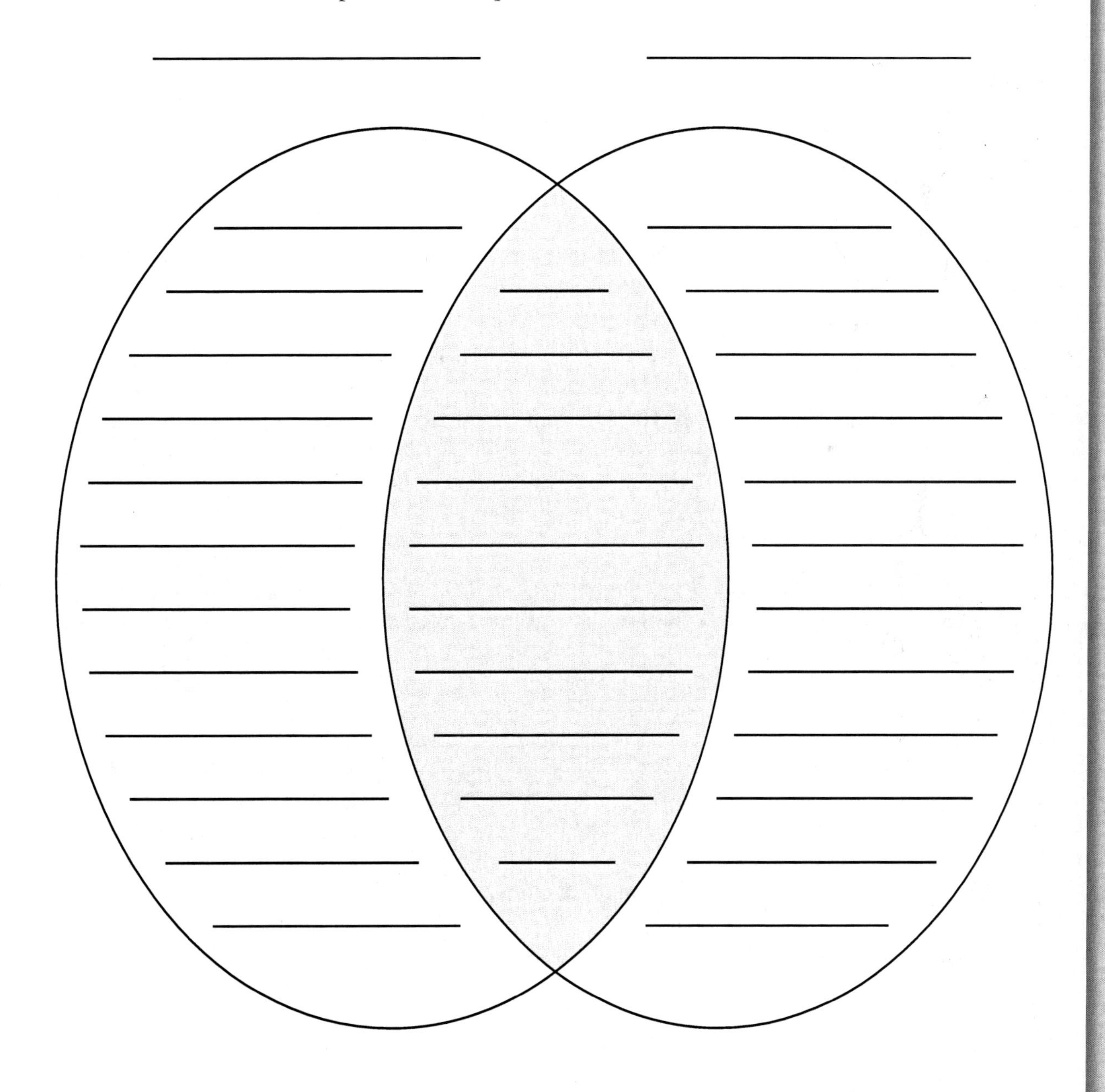

Strategies for Using the Leveled Texts *(cont.)*

Below-Grade-Level Students *(cont.)*

Framed Outline

This is an underused technique that yields great results. Many below-grade-level students struggle with reading comprehension. They need a framework to help them attack the text and gain confidence in comprehending the material. Once students gain confidence and learn how to locate factual information, the teacher can phase out this technique.

There are two steps to successfully using this technique. First, the teacher writes cloze sentences. Second, the students complete the cloze activity and write summary sentences.

Framed Outline Example

Eco-________ are helpful when trying to solve mysteries about ________. To make an ________, you must first collect ________. This information will help you ________ your predictions. Oftentimes, scientists use this ________ to make a ________, ________, or ________. This tool can organize predictions and help ________ figure out a ________. These ________ can become solutions!

Summary Sentences

To make an Eco-prediction, you should be organized and make a plan. First make a prediction, then collect data. You can display this information in a chart, graph or table. These steps will help you monitor your predictions until you reach a solution.

Modeling Written Responses

A frequent concern of educators is that below-grade-level students write poor responses to content-area questions. This problem can be remedied if resource teachers and classroom teachers model what good answers look like. This is a technique you may want to use before asking your students to respond to the comprehension questions associated with the leveled texts in this series.

First, read the question aloud. Then display the question on the board and discuss how you would go about answering the question. Next, write the answer using a complete sentence that accurately answers the question. Repeat the procedure for several questions so that students can understand that written responses are your expectation. To take this one step further, post a variety of responses to a single question. Ask students to identify the strongest response and tell why it is strong. Have students identify the weakest answers and tell why they are weak. By doing this, you are helping students evaluate and strengthen their own written responses.

Strategies for Using the Leveled Texts *(cont.)*

On-Grade-Level Students

Student-Directed Learning

Because they are academically on grade level, student-directed learning activities can serve as a way to build independence and challenge this population of students toward further success. Remember to use the texts in this book as jump starts so that students will be interested in finding out more about the topics. On-grade-level students may enjoy any of the following activities:

- Write your own questions, exchange them with others, and grade each other's responses.
- Review the text and teach the topic to another group of students.
- Read other texts about the topic to further expand your knowledge.
- Create an illustrated timeline or presentation on the topic to present to the class.
- Create your own story similar to the plot in the passage read.
- Lead a discussion group around the leveled question that accompanies the text.
- Research topics from the text in depth and write a new text based on the information.
- Extend the plot of the story or write a new ending to the text.

Highlight It!

Teach students to parse out information based on the genre while they are reading. Use the chart below and a highlighter to focus students on genre-specific text features.

Genre	What do I highlight?
fiction—historical fiction, realistic fiction, literature	characters, problem, setting, solution, theme/moral
nonfiction—biography, autobiography, informational	leading/main idea sentence, important information, sequence of events

Strategies for Using the Leveled Texts *(cont.)*

On-Grade-Level Students *(cont.)*

Detective Work

Teach students to be analytical, like detectives. Direct students' attention to text features such as titles, illustrations, and subheadings by asking students to cover the text and only look at the text features. They can use the chart below to organize analytical thinking about text features prior to reading the text.

Name of Text:		
Text Feature	Why do you think this feature was included?	What can this feature tell you about what the text might be about?
title, subtitle, and headings		
pictures, images, and captions		
diagrams and maps		

Strategies for Using the Leveled Texts *(cont.)*

Above-Grade-Level Students

Open-Ended Questions and Activities

Teachers need to be aware of activities that provide a ceiling that is too low for above-grade-level students. When given activities like this, these students become disengaged. These students can do more, but how much more? Offering open-ended questions and activities will provide above-grade-level students with opportunities to perform at or above their ability levels. For example, ask students to evaluate major events described in the texts, such as: "In what ways do maps help people get around?" or "Explain why civil rights are important for all citizens?" These questions require students to form opinions, think deeply about the issues, and form statements in their minds. Questions like this have lots of right answers.

The generic open-ended question stems listed here can be adapted to any topic. There is one leveled comprehension question for each text in this book. These extension question stems can be used to develop further comprehension questions for the leveled texts.

- In what ways did . . .
- How might you have done this differently . . .
- What if . . .
- What are some possible explanations for . . .
- How does this affect . . .
- Explain several reasons why . . .
- What problems does this create . . .
- Describe the ways . . .
- What is the best . . .
- What is the worst . . .
- What is the likelihood . . .
- Predict the outcome . . .
- Form a hypothesis . . .
- What are three ways to classify . . .
- Support your reason . . .
- Compare this to modern times . . .
- Make a plan for . . .
- Propose a solution to. . .
- What is an alternative to . . .

Strategies for Using the Leveled Texts *(cont.)*

Above-Grade-Level Students *(cont.)*

Tiered Assignments

Teachers can differentiate lessons by using tiered assignments or extension activities. These assignments are designed to have varied levels of depth, complexity, and abstractness. All students work toward one concept or outcome, but the lesson is tiered to allow for different levels of readiness and performance levels. As students work, they build on and extend their prior knowledge and understanding. Guidelines for writing tiered lessons include the following:

1. Pick the skill, concept, or generalization that needs to be learned.
2. Assess the students using classroom discussions, quizzes, tests, or journal entries.
3. Think of an on-grade level activity that teaches this skill, concept, or generalization.
4. Take another look at the activity from Step 3. Modify this activity to meet the needs of the below-grade-level and above-grade-level learners. Add complexity and depth for the above-grade-level learners. Add vocabulary support and concrete examples for the below-grade-level students.

Extension Activities Ideas

Extension activities can be used to extend the reading beyond the passages in this book. These suggested activities will help get you started. (Note: All the passages do not have extension activities.)

1. Research a mystery in history. Write a paragraph about the event and share it with a friend.
2. Construct your own go-kart. First make a blueprint and list the materials you need. Then, construct your go-kart and present it to your class.
3. Pretend you own a restaurant. What items might you include on your menu to ensure your patrons are eating healthy? Create the menu and list the ingredients in each dish.
4. Make a map of your neighborhood on a coordinate grid. Plot and label all the major landmarks that you and your family visit.
5. Research a sea animal. Create a poster with important facts about the animal you chose. Make sure to include its life cycle, predators, and prey.
6. Many cultures prepare and eat special breads. Research 3–4 different cultures and create a bread recipe book. Include the ingredients and steps to make each bread.
7. Imagine you lived during colonial times. Create a journal detailing your daily life for a week. What might you eat? How will you entertain yourself? Get creative and describe your surroundings!
8. What historical figure are you interested in learning more about? Write 10 research questions that you could ask this person. Research to find your answers!
9. Dr. Martin Luther King Jr. was an activist who fought for civil rights. Research another activist. Write a biography of his or her life including key information.

Strategies for Using the Leveled Texts *(cont.)*

English Language Learners

Effective teaching for English language learners requires effective planning. To achieve success, teachers need to understand and use a conceptual framework to help them plan lessons and units. These are the six major components to any framework:

1. **Select and Define Concepts and Language Objectives**—Before having students read one of the texts in this book, first choose a subject/concept and a language objective (listening, speaking, reading, or writing) appropriate for the grade level. The next step is to clearly define the concept to be taught. This requires knowledge of the subject matter, alignment with local and state objectives, and careful formulation of a statement that defines the concept. This concept represents the overarching idea and should be posted in a visible place in the classroom.

   By the definition of the concept, post a set of key language objectives. Based on the content and language objectives, select essential vocabulary from the text. (A list of possible words can be found on page 134.) The number of new words selected should be based on students' English language levels. Post these words on a word wall that may be arranged alphabetically or by themes.

2. **Build Background Knowledge**—Some English language learners may have a lot of knowledge in their native language, while others may have little or no knowledge. Build the background knowledge of the students using different strategies, such as the following:

   Visuals—Use posters, photographs, postcards, newspapers, magazines, drawings, and video clips of the topic you are presenting. The texts in this series include multiple images, maps, diagrams, charts, tables, and illustrations for your use.

   Realia—Bring real-life objects to the classroom. If you are teaching about circuits, bring electronics that use different types of circuits.

   Vocabulary and Word Wall—Introduce key vocabulary in context. Create families of words. Have students draw pictures that illustrate the words and write sentences about the words. Also be sure you have posted the words on a word wall in your classroom. (Key vocabulary from the various texts can be found on page 134.)

   Desk Dictionaries—Have students create their own desk dictionaries using index cards. On one side of each card, they should draw a picture of the word. On the opposite side, they should write the word in their own language and in English.

Strategies for Using the Leveled Texts *(cont.)*

English Language Learners *(cont.)*

3. **Teach Concepts and Language Objectives**—Present content and language objectives clearly. Engage students by using a hook and pace the delivery of instruction, taking into consideration the students' English language levels. State the concept or concepts to be taught clearly. Use the first languages of the students whenever possible, or assign other students who speak the same languages to mentor and to work cooperatively with the English language learners.

   Lev Semenovich Vygotsky (1978), a Russian psychologist, wrote about the zone of proximal development. This theory states that good instruction must fill the gap that exists between the present knowledge of a child and the child's potential. Scaffolding instruction is an important component when planning and teaching lessons. English language learners cannot skip stages of language and content development. You must determine where the students are in the learning process and teach to the next level using several small steps to get to the desired outcome. With the leveled texts in this series and periodic assessment of students' language levels, you can support students as they climb the academic ladder.

4. **Practice Concepts and Language Objectives**—English language learners need to practice what they learn by using engaging activities. Most people retain knowledge best after applying what they learn to their own lives. This is definitely true for English language learners. Students can apply content and language knowledge by creating projects, stories, skits, poems, or artifacts that show what they have learned. Some activities should be geared to the right side of the brain, like those listed above. For students who are left-brain dominant, activities such as defining words and concepts, using graphic organizers, and explaining procedures should be developed. The following teaching strategies are effective in helping students practice both language and content:

   Simulations—Students re-create concepts in texts by becoming a part of them. They have to make decisions as if they lived in historical times. For example, students can pretend that they are colonists. They have to describe and act out the conditions of the colonies in the New World. Or, students can act out a fictional passage by pretending they are Anne of Green Gables. They can reenact the passage while extending their understanding of the main character's personality.

   Literature response—Read a text from this book. Have students choose two people described or introduced in the text. Ask students to write conversations the people might have. Or you can have students write journal entries about events in the daily lives of the important people. Literature responses can also include student opinions, reactions, and questions about texts.

Strategies for Using the Leveled Texts *(cont.)*

English Language Learners *(cont.)*

4. Practice Concepts and Language Objectives *(cont.)*

Have a short debate—Make a controversial statement such as, "Segregation is fair." After reading a text in this book, have students think about the question and take positions based on their points of view. As students present their ideas, you or a student can act as the moderator.

Interview—Students may interview a member of their family or a neighbor to obtain information regarding a topic from the texts in this book. For example: How is your life similar to the lives of colonists in the 1600s and 1700s?

5. Evaluation and Alternative Assessments—Evaluation should be used to inform instruction. Students must have opportunities to show their understandings of concepts in different ways and not only through standard assessments. Use both formative and summative assessments to ensure that you are effectively meeting your content and language objectives. Formative assessment is used to plan effective lessons for particular groups of students. Summative assessment is used to find out how much the students have learned. Other authentic assessments that show day-to-day progress are: text retelling, teacher rating scales, student self-evaluations, cloze statements, holistic scoring of writing samples, performance assessments, and portfolios. Periodically assessing student learning will help you ensure that students continue to receive the correct levels of texts.

6. Home/School Connection—The home/school connection is an important component in the learning process for English language learners. Parents are the first teachers, and they establish expectations for their children. These expectations help shape the behavior of their children. By asking parents to be active participants in the education of their children, students get double doses of support and encouragement. As a result, families become partners in the education of their children, and chances for success in your classroom increase.

You can send home copies of the texts in this series for parents to read with their children. You can even send multiple levels to meet the needs of your second-language parents as well as your students. In this way, you are sharing what you are covering in the classroom with your whole second language community.

Resources

Contents of Digital Resource CD

PDF Files

The full-color PDFs provided are each six pages long and contain all three levels of a reading passage. For example, *History's Mysteries* (pages 23–28) is the *mysteries.pdf* file.

Text Files

The Microsoft Word® documents include the text for all three levels of each reading passage. For example, *History's Mysteries* (pages 23–28) is the *mysteries.docx* file.

Text Title	Text File	PDF
Excerpt from *Anne of Green Gables*	anne.docx	anne.pdf
Excerpt from *The Story of Dr. Dolittle*	dolittle.docx	dolittle.pdf
History's Mysteries	mysteries.docx	mysteries.pdf
Go-Kart Racing	gokart.docx	gokart.pdf
Food Groups	foodgroups.docx	foodgroups.pdf
Eco-Predictions	eco.docx	eco.pdf
Journeys: Land, Air, Sea	journeys.docx	journeys.pdf
Patterns Around Us	patterns.docx	patterns.pdf
All About Sharks	sharks.docx	sharks.pdf
The Bread Book	bread.docx	bread.pdf
Producers and Consumers	prodcon.docx	prodcon.pdf
The Nutrient Cycle	nutrient.docx	nutrient.pdf
Circuits	circuits.docx	circuits.pdf
Sound Waves and Communication	soundwaves.docx	soundwaves.pdf
The Story of Fossil Fuels	fossilfuels.docx	fossilfuels.pdf
Pocahontas	pocahontas.docx	pocahontas.pdf
Life in the Colonies	colonies.docx	colonies.pdf
Marie Antoinette	antoinette.docx	antoinette.pdf
Lewis and Clark	lewisclark.docx	lewisclark.pdf
Dr. Martin Luther King Jr.	mlkjr.docx	mlkjr.pdf

Word Documents of Texts

- Change leveling further for individual students.
- Separate text and images for students who need additional help decoding the text.
- Resize the text for visually impaired students.

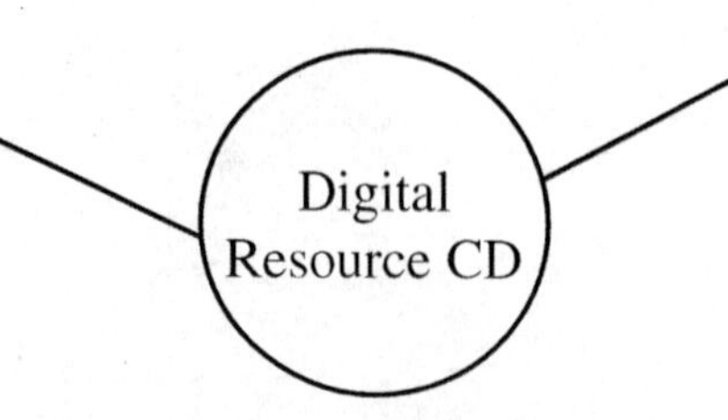

Full-Color PDFs of Texts

- Project texts for whole-class review.
- Post on your website and read texts online.
- Email texts to parents or students at home.